The Wait
"Life and the Wilderness"

BY: KIRK JACKSON

ISBN: 0692682600
ISBN-13: 978-0692682609

DEDICATION

First to the Lord, Jesus Christ.
To my loving wife, Chelsie; my greatest support.
Our amazing children, Nicolas, Lauryn and Sawyer Grace.

CONTENTS

Foreword

By Bill Kohlun

This writing reflects directly from the author's own journey. My relationship with Kirk began in 2005. In the past eleven years I have been witness to not only his wilderness, but also his transformation. His growth has been personal, emotional, physical and, most importantly, spiritual. His wilderness has required change in direction many times, and sacrifices at each and every turning point. Yet, in every instance his eyes have been on the Lord Jesus Christ, steadfast in seeking guidance, humble in his rewards and peacefulness in his trials. This "Wait" should be one of the keys to beginning your wilderness journey. I am humbled to have been a part of Kirk's wilderness.

ACKNOWLEDGMENTS

Thank you to my wife and kids for their patience in the process.
Thank you to my parents, Robert and Loretta, for your unwavering support, leadership and insight.
Special thanks to Bill Kohlun and Stacy Turner for their great help.
Thanks to all the supporting and encouraging family and friends, especially from Rugged.

PREFACE

The wilderness, the part of the story almost everyone knows is coming but hardly anyone wants to talk about. Everyone can tell you the beginning of the story and almost every self-help book highlights where you "should" end up. We have a goal in mind, we are focused on achieving that goal, and whether in business, finances, our own fitness or self-image, nothing will slow us down from that goal. We have all seen "before" and "after" pictures of home renovations or personal fitness stories. The problem is that these images only tell part of the story. Home renovation television shows make the remodeling of a home look much simpler than it really is, and they do it all in about 30 minutes. Much in the same way, exercise products will show you "before" and "after" photos of "satisfied customers" and show you a "simple" exercise routine that anyone can do ten minutes a day, three days a week and realize the same results. These photos are accompanied by video clips of people smiling who seem to be enjoying their workout, and it all seems effortless.

Here's the rub…If you have attempted any of these things in your life, you know that the simple and easy workout is much harder than it seems. You know that getting control of your finances takes more effort than following a few simple steps to financial freedom. In fact, with just about everything between being born and dying (neither of which we can control) there is always a transition time, a time of changing. This transition time is challenging and hard. Many times in the process you have to fight the urge to give up, and the multitudes of reasons—maybe you're not seeing the results you think you should see, maybe the process is more challenging than you expected or the price to finish is higher than you are willing to pay. Whatever your reasoning, you are the only one that can choose to continue. No one can make that decision for you. Those times of transition we will call the wilderness, and as we continue, we will explore the challenges, purposes and necessities of the wilderness times in our lives. So, what are you waiting for Let's get started!

INTRODUCTION

Imagine you are taking a walk on a hiking trail. This trail is not just a single trail. Like most hiking areas, there are several different paths. Depending on how much time and energy you have and where you start, there are many different combinations of paths you can take and still return to where you started. Let's say you have come to this hiking area several times and spent quite a bit of time hiking the different trails, but one day you journey down a trail and come to a split. You are looking at two different options, one to your left and one to your right. You recognize the trail to your left because you have taken it before. The trail to your right has you stopped in your tracks. You have been to this area several times before, but this particular trail seems completely foreign. You realize you have two feelings inside of you. One is encouraging you to just stick with what's familiar, and one is curiously pulling you toward the place you have never been, to experience something new, even if you aren't sure what's beyond your view. So, what do you do?

This is not a trick question, and there is not necessarily a right or wrong answer. This scenario represents times where we often find ourselves in life. Have you ever wondered why the self-help section is so large in book stores? My theory is that it centers around our nature to desire more. People who like to work out will find time and energy to work out more and get stronger. People who want more money will focus their time and energy to try making more money. The same is true with people who want success, organization, financial freedom, etc. I believe this is true in almost every area of our lives. What about serving and following God? Do you treat that part of your life the same? Or is serving and following God simply an accessory in your life? These are questions that deserve time for sincere personal reflection.

Let's take some time right now and understand how we are called as followers of Christ. "Follower of Christ" is an apt description of the call of God to each of us. In Luke 5, Jesus "saw a tax collector named Levi, sitting at the tax booth. And he said to him, 'Follow me.' And leaving everything, he rose and followed Him" (Luke 5:27-28).[1] Over and over again in the gospels, Jesus calls people to follow Him. In Matthew 4, Jesus called His first disciples by saying, "Follow me, and I will make you fishers of men" (Matthew 4:19). In Matthew 10, Jesus says, "And whoever does not take his cross and follow me is not worthy of me" (Matthew 10:38). The idea of following Jesus is the true recognition for our lives as Christians.

Keeping that in mind, let us return to the walking trail where we are at the cross roads. Let me ask the question, what if it is the Holy Spirit that is drawing you toward that unknown trail? Would you go without question, or are there certain conditions and priorities that might keep you from taking that trail? We can find many reasons to avoid it—things like, I have a meeting in about an hour and need to get back. Or, the trail is too dark. The trail is definitely unfamiliar and that could slow you down from the pace you are accustomed to, you reason. The trail may be steeper and sharper than you are used to and push you physically. Besides, you don't know exactly where the trail ends. All these are "reasons" [or excuses] for not going down that unfamiliar trail. (This is not an exhaustive list, but you get the idea.)

Reasons or Excuses? Your entire "following" life, and its effectiveness, will be shaped by what you allow to influence those decisions.

I have always been close to my dad. My dad has been one of my best friends and a person I have always been able to rely on. I have learned, throughout my life, that my dad is a wise man who has experience as a father, husband, leader, and follower of Christ. My dad has never been the type of person to force his opinion or view on me, but has always encouraged me to understand why I make the decisions that I do. He has always encouraged me to make decisions that reflect a deep belief or reason. My dad has never been a fan of excuses. He never let me get away with excuses because he loves me and wants what is best for me. My dad wanted me to grow and be responsible for my own actions, not to rely on using excuses.

There is a stark contrast between reason and excuse. One definition of reason is "good or obvious cause to do something."[11] A good cause for action is a reason such as holding the door open because the person behind you has their hands full; or saying no to scheduling a meeting at noon because you already have a lunch appointment that day. Volunteering to help serve food at the mission because you are available Thursday night. These are just a few examples of "good cause for action." As a general rule, reasons are empowered by love, compassion, obedience, and selflessness.

On the other hand, an excuse is "an explanation put

forward to *defend or justify* a fault or offense. (emphasis mine)"[11] An explanation to defend an action, or inaction, is an excuse. Think of the response of a child involved in an argument or fight who says, "He/She started it!" Maybe you skip going to the gym because you "don't have time" while spending three hours a day watching television. Perhaps it is choosing to take credit for the work your entire group did because you were the leader even though the rest of the team put more time and effort into the project to make it successful. There are so many ways that you defend your actions. Typically, excuses are directly related to selfishness, pride, and arrogance (the exact opposite of "reasons"). Excuses justify your desire to avoid responsibility and remain uncommitted. To remain uncommitted to Christ is characteristic of those who are NOT followers of Christ.

That unfamiliar trail is a great representation where transition, or wilderness, seasons begin in your life. Many of us do our best to avoid coming to this place, this unfamiliar crossroad. Maybe you are one of them. You schedule your life right down to the minute. You are comfortable in the rhythm and pattern of your life. You know what to expect and you have a plan. You are happy with your career, lifestyle, and family, but then God brings you to His unfamiliar trail. How would you respond? In Genesis 12, that is exactly where Abram was. (Genesis 12:1-4 NKJV.)[2]

Abram was with his family in Ur of the Chaldeans, and his father, Terah, took Abram, Sarai (Abram's wife) and Lot (Terah's grandson and Abram's nephew), and headed toward Canaan. (The scripture never says why they decided to make this move and it doesn't really matter because Terah is not the focus of the story.) Along their journey they had stopped in Haran, and there Terah dies at 205 years of age. Genesis 12:1 says, "Now the Lord had said to Abram: 'Get out of your country,'" (Genesis 12:1a NKJV). We are going to explore this idea a little more later on, but isn't it intriguing that the Lord had said to Abram indicating that Abram and the Lord had already had this conversation? Notice that we are only 12 chapters into the Bible at this point and God says "Get out of your country" (Genesis 12:1 NKJV). In today's language, God just told Abram to leave all the comforts of home, to leave his retirement fund behind, and to leave his daily routine. God asked Abram to leave his familiar, safe, predictable trail and to follow Him down this unfamiliar trail. Abram has no idea where it leads and how uncomfortable it may be. A couple of verses later we learn, "Abram departed as the Lord had spoken to him, Lot went with him. And Abram was seventy-five years old when he departed from Haran" (Genesis 12:4 NKJV).

Abram chose to weigh all the "reasons" not to follow God and in the end chose the unfamiliar trail. I would ask you, where in your life do you feel God, through the Holy Spirit, encouraging you to take the first steps away from the familiar, convenient trail onto the unfamiliar trail and into the wilderness? Will you choose to allow God's voice to outweigh all the reasons to stay on the familiar path? Are you weighing out whether what you are feeling could be classified as "reasons", or have you considered they might be "excuses"?

CHAPTER 1
THE WILDERNESS

What image comes to your mind when you think of the wilderness? Is it desert? Is it rain forest? Is it a strange, unfamiliar city or town? Is it a distant country? The reality is that the wilderness could be any of these places. The examples we will be talking about are literal wilderness experiences, and if you are experiencing this, it may be that the Holy Spirit is leading you toward a wilderness of your own. Do not easily dismiss the reality that the wilderness in your own life may not take you around the world or to a far off place. The idea of the wilderness, or the unfamiliar trail, is not as much about a physical place but is primarily about transition. You have to understand that in this life we are continually in transition. However, there are times in life that the transition is more pronounced or more drastic than at other times. Looking back to the call to "follow" Christ, we must recognize that in order to follow Him, we must leave everything behind and follow Jesus' lead—just like the original disciples. That is the essence of the words of Peter in Acts 2 when he said, "Repent and be baptized every one of you in the name of Jesus Christ for the forgiveness of your sins, and you will receive the gift of the Holy Spirit" (Acts 2:38). The word repent in this context is to turn from your old ways of thinking, to trust in something different than you have trusted in up to this time.[13] This is essentially what you are being asked to do each day that God leads you down the unfamiliar path. God is asking you to stop trusting yourself and your own understanding and to trust Him. (Proverbs 3:5-8.) Ultimately, as followers of Christ, shouldn't our entire life be a continual trip down the unfamiliar path? To truly be followers of Christ, our response to His call "to follow me" is not a onetime thing but a continual following. We have to trust Him completely and continually every single day and as Proverbs says, "He will make straight your paths" (Proverbs 3:6). Since we are playing follow the leader, and Jesus is the leader, then how does Jesus get us to the wilderness in our lives? There are many answers to this question, but we will look at these specifically: betrayal, persecution, rebellion, and

Holy Spirit leading. There are different ways of finding yourself in the wilderness, but be encouraged that God is going to use your wilderness time for your good.

Betrayal

Everyone is part of a family. No one gets to choose their family. The decision of the family someone is born into is God's alone. Unfortunately, God doesn't consult with you before you are born into your family. Some families are wealthy and privileged, while other families are poor and destitute. Some families are dysfunctional and full of hate, while other families are in sync and extremely loving. Families consist of alcoholics, movie stars, politicians, murderers, drug dealers, pastors, or garbage collectors...and the list goes on and on. The fact of the matter is, you didn't get to choose your family or when you were born because that is what God chose for you. That doesn't make one situation right and one wrong.

Understanding that, let's look at a boy named Joseph. Most likely, Joseph was born into a family a little different than yours. His father had four wives and from those four wives Joseph's father had twelve sons. So Joseph had eleven brothers, ELEVEN! I have three brothers; I could not imagine having eight more. My brothers and I had some good fights and arguments through the years, but I'm sure we never got close to the tension in Joseph's house with twelve emerging men living under one roof. When Joseph was seventeen years old he gave a bad report about his brothers to his father. (Genesis 37:1-28.) Verse 29 tells us that Joseph was his father's favorite and so he made Joseph a coat of many colors. Joseph's father gave him a gift that was for him to wear every day and let everyone know he was the favorite. Now his brothers don't like him at all and can't even find nice words to say about him. Then Joseph has a dream whose basic interpretation is that he was going to rule over his brothers (all but one older than he was) and his parents too. His father sends him to check on the brothers who hate him, and they see him coming and decided to kill him. Again, my brothers and I have had some pretty significant fights but I would not think about killing any one of my brothers. Joseph's family situation is definitely bad at this point. The brothers beat him up, are talked out of killing him by the only brother who had a sense of reason, and decide instead to put him in a hole, eventually selling him into slavery. They smeared goat's blood on Joseph's cherished coat and took it back to their father, telling him that Joseph had been attacked and killed. This is a harsh way to suddenly find yourself in the wilderness; betrayed by your own brothers, the family you had trusted. Many people have been betrayed by the people they trusted and now find themselves in the wilderness. Consider the life of a young woman raped by a member of her family. She can't bear the shame and hurt, and finally has decided to run away. She is in the wilderness. A man with a promising career chooses to start a business with a good friend only to find himself a few years later without a business or a job because his business partner has scammed the system. He is in the wilderness. A wife and mother finds herself suddenly alone because her unfaithful husband has left his responsibilities. She is in the wilderness. There are many situations that force people into an unexpected wilderness because, like Joseph, they were betrayed by the people closest to them.

At this point, it would be easy to look to God and blame Him for allowing you to be in this place, to wonder why He has forgotten you and to think that God has betrayed you. Let me tell you, God has not forgotten you. God has not betrayed you. He is still almighty and sovereign, but He gave us our own free will. The self-destruction and betrayal that has sent you into this wilderness is human nature. For some of you this wilderness is relief. Yes, it is scary, but not in the same way as the situation that you came from. For those of you who find yourself in an abusive situation or fresh out of an abusive situation, the wilderness is truly a relief, a relief that you may have been hoping and praying for over weeks, months, or even years. For others, the wilderness came out of nowhere and brings an array of feelings that include: doubt, disbelief, anger, frustration, fear, or anxiety. No matter who betrayed you or how you were betrayed, however you find yourself in the wilderness through betrayal, you have a choice to make. Will you continue to carry the pain of the past all through your wilderness? Will you allow God to forgive you and free you from your past by forgiving those who betrayed you and sent you to the wilderness? Will you be willing to forgive yourself for getting into the situation in the first place?

Persecution

Remember that everyone is born into a family and a specific situation, not by their choice but by the hand and choice of God. Some people are born into and experience betrayal. Others are born into a world of persecution and slavery. Unfortunately, in many places in the world persecution and slavery is reality. In America, we had division in our country over whether or not it was acceptable to "own" another human being, just 150 years ago. In some countries in the world like Rwanda, during the country's civi war, the tribe or family you were born into determined which side of a fight for control of your country you were on and where you were accepted. In some parts of the world, even today, being born into families of certain ethnicities or religions makes you a target. Throughout human history, until relatively recent times, slavery was a common practice around the world. You have to understand there are different types of slavery, or servant hood, that we see throughout cultures and times. Much of the Roman culture did have slaves but that was not the same as slavery of more modern times. The Roman "slaves" were more servants in modern context. These "slaves" often had their own property, family, and homes. In more recent times, people in slavery were treated as property of another. So if they had children, they were not their own. Their children were the property of the slave owner. This more modern version of slavery can lend itself toward violence and mistreatment. It is that type of slavery that was developing in Exodus, and the people of Israel were the slaves. Exodus 1:13 says, "So they ruthlessly made the people of Israel work as slaves." This may be the picture of your life, enslaved by circumstances against your will. Waking up every day in fear of what the day may bring, genuinely fearing the next moment, or even your mother and/or father. This is a reality that some are blinded to, but not God. God is very aware of where you are, and He says, "The Lord works righteousness and justice for all who are oppressed" (Psalm 103:6). Psalm 146:7 says, "The Lord sets the prisoners free;" God knows that is exactly how you feel, like a prisoner in your own life, in a prison that you did not choose for yourself, persecuted and suffering.

You may ask, how do you know that God knows my suffering? How do you know that God hears my cries for this suffering to end? Because God said that about His people! Moses encounters a bush that is burning but not consumed. As if that isn't strange enough, God speaks to Moses from that bush. God said to Moses, "I have surely seen the affliction of my people...I know their sufferings, and I have come down to deliver them" (Exodus 3:7-8). Rest assured, God sees your suffering and His desire is to deliver you from it. God's desire for His people was to lead them out of Egypt and into Canaan, a place God called "good and large", "flowing with milk and honey" (Exodus 3:8 NKJV). I believe God's desire for you is the same, to take you to a place of rest from your slavery and persecution. But there is a catch. In order to leave the slavery, there is resistance from the task master (the owner) which has to be dealt with before you can leave. That resistance can only be overcome by the power of God because only God can free you from that situation. When He does, you will be standing at the edge of the wilderness! You must decide in this wilderness to separate yourself from the practices of slavery that you were in before, to forgive those who enslaved you, and to follow

God alone. Will you choose to follow only God? Will you allow yourself to forgive?

Rebellion

We have seen, in betrayal and persecution, how the path to the wilderness time in your life is one that you may look forward to because it offers a respite to your situation. Now we have come to a completely different situation. You are born into a family, in a culture or society that is completely out of your control, but there is also a nature with which you are born. You are born with a nature of sin, rebellion, and self-destruction. If you don't believe me you probably have not observed children very much. I have a son and two daughters and I can assure you there are many things in their lives that I have not had to teach them. For example, I did not have to teach my children to lie. Once they learned to talk, they learned to blame someone else. As good and loving parents, my wife and I set boundaries and have rules in our home that have consequences. And just like every home, those rules and boundaries are tested on a daily basis. Do you think our kids test the boundaries because they are unaware that we have rules at our house? Or could it be that they were born with a predisposition to fight against what is good for them? Even though we have rules at our house, we do offer grace pretty frequently. Usually that exchange goes something like this, "Do you know why you are in trouble?"

"Yes, because I messed up my brother's Legos on purpose."

"You know what the consequences would normally be, but I'm going to give you grace this time. Do you know what grace is?"

"Yes, it is getting something I don't deserve."

"That's right. I suggest you apologize to your brother and help him rebuild his Lego creations."

The context of this conversation is a recognition that they did something wrong and they have shown remorse and are genuinely apologetic. There are times, shockingly enough, that my children not only do something they know breaks the rules of our home, but continue to break that rule. My job as a loving father is to show them I love them and let them know that rules are in place for their good. This is never a pleasant interaction for me or my children, but it is a loving one. I discipline my children because I love them. God does the same thing with you and me. "Those whom I love, I reprove and discipline" (Revelation 3:19a).

When we rebel against God, often times He will lead us into the wilderness specifically to get our attention. In Hosea, God is speaking to his people about their rebellion. They have continued to choose other gods and continued in their rebellion against Him. God has tried to get their attention and He has extended grace over years of rebellion. God's charge against His people finishes with "they went after her lovers and forgot me" (Hosea 2:13b). God has just finished His rebuke of Israel and talked about how He would judge His people. He explained to them how they had broken His rules and acted in rebellion against Him. Then the very next verse says, "Therefore, behold, I will allure her, and bring her into the wilderness, and speak tenderly to her" (Hosea 2:14). God's response to His people's disobedience wasn't complete destruction, it was leading them into the wilderness. You may be in this place of continual rebellion against God. You may be resisting God and trying to avoid Him. If that is you, don't be surprised when He takes you out into the wilderness. In this wilderness, God is taking you as His child for correction and for you to hear Him and remember His voice.

There is another way to get to the wilderness through rebellion. In this story it's not called the wilderness, it's called the distant country. In Luke 15, we find the parable of the prodigal son. (Luke 15:11-32.) This son took all of his inheritance and he chose to leave and go into the distant country. While he was in the distant country he spent his money on wild living. We aren't told this, but there were definitely signs that things were not going well for him. He surely had less money after every party. Then he completely ran out of money. That's usually a sign that things haven't gone well. Next, a severe famine comes and he finds himself in need. He has gone from having everything he could ever want or need at home, to finding himself going without. This son didn't find himself here over night and no one else made him go there. He chose this life. Just like so many after him have been lured into the party life and all its promises, many of them have ignored all the warning signs along the way until they have nothing left. That is exactly where the prodigal son found himself in the distant country, a wilderness, of his own choosing. The reality is, that in the distant country, unlike the other wilderness experiences, you are separated from God because of your sin. Separation from God is being spiritually dead and God's Word deals with this often. Romans 6 says, "The wages of sin is death" (Romans 6:23a). Proverbs tells us, "There is a way that seems right to a man, but its end is the way of death" (Proverbs 14:12 NKJV). Over and over again, the Word of God speaks of separation from God. This means eternal death. The only way to leave the distant country is to be brought back to life; to be welcomed in by the Father. You were made to be in relationship with God. You are either running away in rebellion or you are running to Him through repentance. Remember that repentance is a change of direction. Repenting and turning from the old ways and idols, turning instead toward God and pursuing Him alone.

Holy Spirit leading

We were all born at one time or another. Every person has a date of birth. This statement is evident, because it is impossible for you to be reading this right now without being alive. From the very moment of your birth you have had the very same nature of rebellion as anyone, even my kids. That very same tendency to hurt yourself, hurt other people, and take no responsibility for it. Once we reached an age where we knew the difference between right and wrong we were officially separated from God. From that moment on we were alive in our flesh, or humanness, but we were dead in Christ. (John 3:18 NKJV.) This is exactly the narrative we enter in John 3. (John 3:1-8.) Nicodemus, a religious leader, comes at night to Jesus. He comes to Jesus at night because he isn't ready to publicly follow Jesus, but his curiosity pulls him in. Nicodemus comes and says, "Rabbi, we know that You are a teacher come from God; for no one can do these signs that You do unless God is with him" (John 3:2 NKJV). Nicodemus opens up by calling Jesus Rabbi (or teacher) and follows by declaring "we" know you have come from God. Do you think he really knew what he was saying? If he did, he could not have been prepared for Jesus' response. Jesus said, "unless one is born again, he cannot see the kingdom of God" (John 3:3 NKJV). Pardon me? Nicodemus had just told Jesus he believed he was from God, and his response was you must be born again to see the kingdom of God! Remember that Nicodemus was born physically and his only understanding of being born was physical. Nicodemus responds in terms of physical birth, and Jesus clarifies by saying, "that which is born of the flesh is flesh, and that which is born of the Spirit is spirit" (John 3:6). You were born of the flesh, just like Nicodemus, and because you were born from flesh you are flesh. Flesh is temporary and deals with life as temporary. You eat and your body is satisfied for a little while, but hunger returns. You drink and your thirst is satisfied for a little while, but you will be thirsty again soon. Flesh is led by the flesh. From the moment you are born, your flesh wants to be satisfied. Your natural body leads you to natural food. But what about your spirit? Unless you have been born of the Spirit, your spirit is dead. That's what Jesus is telling Nicodemus. The same thing Paul communicates in Ephesians 2. "And you were dead in the trespasses and sins" (Ephesians 2:1). You are spiritually dead until you are born again of the Spirit! 1 John 1:9 says, "If we confess our sins, He is faithful and just to forgive us our sins and to cleanse us from all unrighteousness." Titus 2 says,

"For the grace of God has appeared, bringing salvation for all people" (Titus 2:11). That is the picture Nicodemus could not see. Jesus put Nicodemus face to face with the idea that unless he is saved from himself, he was hopeless to escape being separated from God. Unless you have declared Jesus as Lord of your life, you are separated from God. Unless you are saved, rescued from your flesh, you will die separated from God. But when you choose to follow Jesus, "old things have passed away; behold, all things have become new" (2 Corinthians 5:17b NKJV). You have been rescued from your fleshly nature and have been given a new nature. All things have become new. You have been born again, this time not of flesh but of the Spirit. The flesh is no longer leading. The Holy Spirit is the leader. You aren't driven by flesh toward temporary things, but instead are directed by the Spirit to the eternal things of the Spirit. Following the Spirit can, and probably will, lead you down the wilderness path.

This wilderness path is different in many ways than the others. The Spirit leading us into the wilderness is not necessarily about sin, correction, or freeing you from bondage, but it could be. This wilderness path is fully about trusting God and following Jesus completely. You have been made new, reborn, by the Holy Spirit. You have declared yourself a follower of Jesus, which means HE is the leader, and where the Spirit leads you is the right place. It also means that when HE leads and where HE leads you have chosen to follow. That is the essence of Luke 9:23, "And He said to all, 'if anyone would come after me, let him deny himself and take up his cross daily and follow me." You have to make a daily choice to follow Jesus. Will you make a daily choice to die to yourself? Will you make a daily choice to live in the Spirit? Will you make a daily choice for Jesus to truly be the leader?

One way or another, you have come to the crossroads of the familiar and unfamiliar paths. The next step you take is important. If you choose to accept the call of Jesus, you will be changed. You will see that the wilderness and unfamiliar time in your life is not just scary and painful, but also exciting and necessary.

CHAPTER 2
STEPPING INTO THE WILDERNESS

Back at the crossroads of the familiar and unfamiliar paths, you are faced with a decision. Will you allow yourself to let go of the familiar? Will you embrace the challenge and reward of stepping into the unknown? You have decided to start down the unfamiliar path. You are willing to explore just a little bit, but if it gets too hard or takes too long you still have the ability to turn back. You are curious about the unfamiliar path but not fully committed to it. You are willing to head toward the unknown but under *your* conditions. This is how many people follow Christ. They are willing to follow Christ as long He fits into their life. They have prayed a prayer and confessed Jesus as Lord, but their life is not much different than it used to be. The call of Jesus is not to follow Him as long as it's convenient. Jesus didn't say He was A way, He said, "I am THE way, THE truth, and THE life. NO ONE comes to the Father except through ME" (John 14:6 NKJV, emphasis mine). This is not the communication of a following of convenience. This is an exclusive relationship. This was not a new idea in terms of relating to God. In the Old Testament, the Tabernacle is where God's presence stayed, in the Most Holy Place. You can read about the Tabernacle and its construction in Exodus chapters 36-40. To enter the presence of God—to enter the Tabernacle—there was only one entrance, the East Gate. The East Gate was the only way to enter a relationship with God. There was no other way. Jesus spoke of Himself as the only way to God. You have read about Jesus saying, "Unless one is born again, he cannot see the kingdom of God" (John 3:3 NKJV). "If anyone would come after me, let him deny himself and take up his cross daily and follow me" (Luke 9:23). These teachings of Jesus speak of total commitment and trusting Him as the only way, just like in John 14:6. You may still think, "I can take a few steps down the unfamiliar trail and check it out, and after I get a better idea of what is down that trail, I will come back when I'm really ready." This sounds like wisdom; if, in fact, you actually come back. The reality is, if you don't take the step now you may avoid taking the trail at all. You may get busy and forget the trail exists. You may be living in a way that is contrary to God and find yourself back on the rebellion trail. This is what Jesus has to say about it: "Jesus said, 'Follow me.' But the man said, "Lord, let me first go and bury my father." And Jesus said to him, 'Leave the dead to bury their own dead. But as for you, go and proclaim the kingdom of God'" (Luke 9:59-60). That seems pretty harsh. Jesus just told a man, don't worry about burying your father. For clarity, we don't know if this guy's father was dying or not. We are not told whether he is young or old. We just know that Jesus told him, "Leave the dead to bury their own dead" (Luke 9:60). Jesus was speaking of the cost of following Him, but He didn't stop there. "Yet another said, 'I will follow you, Lord, but let me first say farewell to those at my home.' Jesus said to him, 'No one who puts his hand to the plow and looks back is fit for the kingdom of God'" (Luke 9:61-62). This is exactly the mentality you would have if you are saying, "let me check out the trail and go get the supplies I need to be really ready." Your desire may be to get everything in order and then follow God, but His word says that's not good enough. We might react just like these two men, telling Jesus, "I'm going to get all the right supplies and then I'll be ready to go," as if Jesus could not be our total supply.

Needed Supplies

It is absolutely normal for you to have a desire to be prepared for a journey. After all, if you were going on a weekend camping trip, you wouldn't want to get all the way to your camping site and find out you didn't bring a tent or food. You would find yourself miles from civilization, without food or shelter. I completely understand not being prepared, having done a few construction projects in my life. If there is anything I have learned in this process, it is to bring all the supplies you need; measure twice and cut once. The last thing you want to do is get close to finishing the project and be in need of more supplies. This has happened to me many times. I have made wrong cuts and had to go get more wood. I have run out of nails or screws. I have needed different tools to complete the project. I'm guessing you understand that feeling and don't want to find yourself in that place either. After all, Jesus did say, "For which of you, desiring to build a tower, does not first sit down and count the cost, whether he has enough to complete it" (Luke 14:28)? Does that justify your actions to prepare? Does that justify your desire to make sure you have enough in your accounts before heading down the unfamiliar trail of moving your family and leaving your job? Does that make your decision to wait until your kids have moved out to go back to college? What about the decision you are delaying? Does that scripture give you relief? Do you feel like you are justified in waiting to be obedient to God? You must read what Jesus said before that. "Whoever does not bear his own cross and come after me cannot be my disciple. For which of you, desiring to build a tower, does not first sit down and count the cost, whether he has enough to complete it" (Luke 14:27-28)? Jesus' teaching of counting the cost was in the same context as putting your hand to the plow. Jesus doesn't encourage you to count the cost of following Him so you can gather enough resources to accomplish it. Jesus speaks of the cost of following Him so you can choose to follow Him completely. You already have all the supplies you need to follow Jesus.

Go back to Genesis chapter 12 and see what Abram took with him. "Then Abram took Sarai his wife and Lot his brother's son, and all their possessions that they had gathered, and the people whom they had acquired in Haran, and they departed to go to the land of Canaan" (Genesis 12:5 NKJV). Abram, considered the father of the Jewish faith and the Christian faith, did not check out his map to see the distance between Haran and Canaan. He did not research how much houses and property cost in Canaan. Abram did not count the cost of following God to Canaan so that he could get everything in order and make sure he had all the supplies necessary to make the move. Abram weighed the reasons to stay and chose to take what he had and follow God to Canaan. This is the heart of what Jesus is saying in Luke 14 as well. Jesus is telling you, and me, that the supplies we need to follow Him we already possess. Take up your cross daily. To follow Jesus, the only needed supplies are crucifying your flesh daily and putting one foot in front of the other with your mind focused on Jesus. Those are the supplies you need for the journey ahead. Are you willing to lay down your life to follow God in this way? When you hear Jesus speak to you about following Him and laying down your own life, isn't it becoming more and more clear that Jesus leading you down the unfamiliar path is more an eventuality than a possibility?

What to expect in the wilderness

My wife, Chelsie, and I lived in Colorado Springs for two years with our three kids. During that time, most of our family lived in Oklahoma. In order for us to go see them, we would typically drive a 10-12 hour trip one way. While every trip we took was a little different, there were some things we could expect every time. We were going to drive all the way to wherever we were staying. We were going to have to make some stops along the way. It was not going to be as comfortable as home. You can expect these same things with your wilderness trail as well.

You are going to walk the unfamiliar trail all the way to the end. Abram had to leave Haran and go all the way to Canaan. The people of Israel left slavery in Egypt and had to go all the way to the Promised Land. You, as a follower of Jesus, are going to have to choose to follow Jesus until the end of your life. What if Abram had decided that Canaan was too far for him to go? What if Abram tried to bargain with God and settled in a different country instead? Would it have been good enough? Is good enough...good enough for God? As a follower of Jesus, if Jesus is still walking and still moving, shouldn't you be still walking and moving? Remember Jesus did say, "Whoever does not bear his own cross and come after me cannot be my disciple" (Luke 14:27). This speaks of complete surrender. It speaks to our desire to stop just short of the finish line. But tell me, what would happen in my family trip if we stopped 100 miles short of our destination? We would not be there yet. We would not get to the place we intended and needed to be. We would be separated from our family. This is why Hebrews encourages us to, "run with endurance the race that is set before us" (Hebrews 12:1b NKJV). Run the race with endurance! Don't give up! Keep putting one foot in front of another until you reach the end. Why would we stop following Christ? Why would you risk separation from Jesus Himself?

You are going to have some pit stops along the way. There are going to be places in your journey through the wilderness that you stop and set up camp. You may stay in that place for a day or two, maybe even longer. If you take a look at the book of Exodus, from the twelfth chapter on, you see their journey through the wilderness. This was a very long journey that took 40 years to complete. The people of Israel had gathered everything they had in Egypt and even plundered the possessions of the Egyptians on their way out of town. (Exodus 12:36) Men, women, and children all heading to their promised land, but no one knew the way because not one of them had ever been there. They had been in Egypt for 400 years. They needed a guide. They needed someone to follow. God told them to follow Him. He would lead them as a pillar of cloud during the day and a pillar of fire at night. When the pillar stopped, the people of Israel didn't just stare at it and wait. They set up their tents and rested. God allowed time to make some pit stops. Your journey down the unfamiliar path will be the same. When you follow Jesus through the wilderness, you will find times that He stops you and allows you rest. He will give you a respite. On a cross country trip, you need a bathroom break. On some trips, you need a talking break. If you are traveling around the world, you need to get up and stretch your legs. You need the layover time. When you are on the journey of following Jesus daily, there will be times that Jesus stops you and just lets you enjoy His presence. He provides you a refreshing drink of living water that only He can provide. Along the way you can expect Jesus, who loves you, to care enough about you to give you rest when you need it.

As you follow Jesus into the wilderness, you can also expect that it won't be as comfortable as home. In Colorado Springs, my family lived in a 3 bedroom home. We had a living room, a dining room and a kitchen. Along with bathrooms and closets—not unusual for an American home. However, in the car on a road trip, with clothing and supplies for five there are few comforts of home. No microwave to warm up food. No personal space to just have some peace and quiet. Imagine the longest trip you have ever taken. Now, think of the feeling when you returned home to your space, your bed, and your things. Think of the life of the people of Israel. The only home they had known was in Egypt. They had taken everything they had and headed out into the great unknown, following God toward a new place to call home. Do you know what they complained about the most in the wilderness? Not having the "comforts" of Egypt. They continually said things like, "you have brought us out into this wilderness to kill this whole assembly with hunger" (Exodus 16:3). And, "Why is it you have brought us up out of Egypt, to kill us and our children and our livestock with thirst" (Exodus 17:3 NKJV)? The people of Israel were blaming Moses for bringing them out of Egypt and leading them to the place they were. Even though they had lived in slavery in Egypt, couldn't own property, and were subject to someone else's orders, they missed it! They complained because they missed the familiar, even though it was not good. They were very uncomfortable in their situation. Remember the nature you were born with—hurting yourself, hurting others, and taking no responsibility for your actions? You will deal with that in your wilderness time. I know you will, because I have personally experienced it in my wilderness times. I have had arguments with my wife that, when we got to the root of the fight, were a result of being uncomfortable in trusting God. She had done nothing wrong. She had not forced me to follow Jesus in this way. I made the choice of my own free will. Yes, I had to apologize and ask her forgiveness. I had to deal with what God was exposing in me through the uncomfortable, wilderness time. You will find yourself in the same place. You will be uncomfortable, stretched and maybe even frustrated. You will lash out at those on the journey with you, for no apparent reason. If you will use the time and patience necessary to fight it out, you will find it is something in your life that Jesus is working you through to make you more like Him. Don't run from the uncomfortable. Don't despise the uncomfortable. Embrace the necessity of the uncomfortable in your life.

The things you can expect in the wilderness probably don't really sound that inviting to you right now. But if you will trust Jesus, He will not disappoint you and Him leading you down the unfamiliar trail isn't without a promise.

CHAPTER 3
THE PROMISE OF THE WILDERNESS TRAIL

Before we left on any of our family trips from Colorado to Oklahoma, we had a promise. We had a destination in mind. We had a purpose for our trip. Our trips to Oklahoma didn't happen by accident. No family vacation happens by accident. No journey into the wilderness happens by accident. The choice to step over into the wilderness is not a blind and hopeless choice. It wasn't a blind choice for the people of Israel, or Abram, and it is not for you. The focus of the choice to enter the wilderness was about what was beyond the wilderness. Stepping into the wilderness was a step of faith. It was the first step in putting the old things behind and pursuing the new things God had promised that lie on the other side of the wilderness. Abram was given a promise to begin the journey toward Canaan. God said, "And I will make you a great nation, and I will bless you and make your name great, so that you will be a blessing" (Genesis 12:2). There is more to this promise, but this establishes that there was a promise for Abram to go into the unknown. Abram was being asked to follow God. We know that God was leading Abram to Canaan. But, according to scripture, Abram did not know. Put yourself in Abram's place. Would you have the faith to follow God "to the land I (God) will show you"? (Genesis 12:1, emphasis mine) Remember that some translations of the Bible say, "The Lord HAD said to Abram" (Genesis 12:1 NKJV, emphasis mine). We don't have any indication if that means repeatedly said. We don't know if Abram's action was immediate. We don't know if God told Abram and he wrestled with the decision for a while. I know in my life when God says, "Follow me, I'll let you know when we get there," I'm looking for some confirmation. I'm asking the Lord to be clear to me so that I am not mistaking His voice with something else. If Abram was like me, chances are there was at least a little delay between God's instruction and Abram's action. Regardless of when Abram acted, the promise God made to Abram was still valid. If Abram would act in obedience, God would bless him so that he would be a blessing.

The people of Israel were given a promise as well. God told Moses from the burning bush, "I have said I will bring you up out of the affliction of Egypt...to a land flowing with milk and honey" (Exodus 3:17 NKJV). This was the message for Moses to tell the people of Israel. Moses was chosen by God, from the back side of the desert, to lead the people of Israel out of slavery in Egypt and into the Promised Land. God promised the people of Israel that He would exchange their hurt, pain, and affliction for a large and good land. Again, God has given His people an amazing promise of what they will find if they trust Him and follow Him. Again, the promise is on the other side of the wilderness. Moses responds exactly how I respond most often when God urges me in the direction of the unfamiliar trail. Moses tried to let God know he wasn't the guy for the job. Moses was standing at the crossroads of the familiar trail and the unfamiliar trail. Just like you, he hesitated to take the first step down the unfamiliar trail. The first step is always hardest. If it was easy it wouldn't be unfamiliar or unknown. If following Jesus was easy, everyone would be following Jesus. "For the gate is narrow and the way is hard that leads to life, and those who find it are few" (Matthew 7:14). Jesus said the way is hard and few people find it. You have to understand following Jesus is not the easy road. Following Jesus is not natural. Following Jesus is challenging in every area of your life, but the promise He gives us is worth every second of discomfort and hardship.

Jesus regularly talks of life and death, or destruction. We just read part of Matthew 7 that in full says, "Enter by the narrow gate. For the gate is wide and the way is easy that leads to destruction, and those who enter by it are many. For the gate is narrow and the way is hard that leads to life, and those who find it are few" (Matthew 7:13-14). In John 10 Jesus says, "I am the door. If anyone enters by me, he will be saved, and will go in and out and find pasture. The thief does not come except to steal, and to kill, and to destroy. I have come that they may have life, and that they may have it more abundantly" (John 10:9-10 NKJV). Jesus is the door! Jesus is the narrow gate! Jesus is the only way into a relationship with God. When you follow Jesus and accept His offer of a relationship with God, you are saved; saved from yourself, saved from your nature of rebellion. You are saved from the wide gate that leads to destruction. This is only the beginning of the promise. It is not enough just to be free from death and destruction. Jesus exchanges that death and destruction and offers life in its place. Jesus said He came that you may have LIFE. This is not a new message from God. God didn't just wake up one day and decide to send Jesus to us to proclaim life. This was His heart for His people all the time. Look back to Deuteronomy and you see that God has positioned the people of Israel at the edge of the Promised Land. God is reminding His people of His heart for them. In Deuteronomy 30, you read words echoed in Jesus' teachings nearly 1500 years later. "I have set before you life and death, blessing and cursing; therefore choose life, that both you and your descendants may live; that you may love the Lord your God, that you may obey His voice, and that you may cling to Him, for He is your life and the length of your days" (Deuteronomy 30:19b-20a NKJV). Choose life! Choose Jesus! Follow Him down the unfamiliar path through the wilderness. Follow Jesus and obey His voice. No, the wilderness is not easy, but Jesus IS your life. Jesus is your promise on the other side of the wilderness.

If death is eternal separation from God, then life is being in the presence of God eternally. But how do we get there? Jesus refers to His followers as sheep and Himself as a shepherd in John chapter 10. "The sheep hear His voice, and He calls His own sheep by name and leads them out. When He has brought out all His own, He goes before them, and the sheep follow Him, for they know His voice" (John 10:3-4). If you get this picture of your relationship with Jesus then it could completely change the way you follow Him. Jesus has called you by name and led you out of the way of death and destruction. When He has called you by name, out of that place, what does He call you to? To follow Him.

Where? Yes! That doesn't make any sense. But it does. Do I follow Him to Africa? Yes! Do I follow Him if He tells me to abandon my suburban life for ministry in the inner city? Yes! What if He leads me to...? Yes! When you follow Jesus and you hear His voice in front of you, the answer is follow Him, and the answer is always Yes. Follow Him completely, until the end of your days on earth. Let the testimony of your life be, "the time of my departure has come. I have fought the good fight, I have finished the race, I have kept the faith" (2 Timothy 4:6b-7). There is promise of life and freedom as you walk in the wilderness. God will use your time on the unfamiliar path—the narrow path—for you to, "lay aside every weight, and sin which clings so closely" (Hebrews 12:1). When you faithfully follow Jesus with endurance, to the end of your days on earth, you will receive eternal life.

Count The Cost

At this time, I would encourage you to make that choice to follow God into the wilderness, and to take that first step down the unfamiliar trail. However, I'm continually being brought back to Luke 14:28, "For which of you, intending to build a tower, does not sit down first and count the cost, whether he has enough to finish it" (NKJV)? Let's hit the brakes and put into context the cost of following Jesus and entering the wilderness. "The kingdom of heaven is like treasure hidden in a field, which a man found and covered up. Then in his JOY he goes and sells all that he has and buys that field" (Matthew 13:44, emphasis mine). Take just a moment and think about that verse. Think about what Jesus is communicating with those words.

Really take the time to think about the implications of that verse.

Jesus just told you that God's kingdom is so valuable that you should willingly, joyfully sell everything you have to purchase it. The cost of the kingdom of heaven could be selling every possession that you own; it could mean selling your home, your car, your furniture, your stocks and stock options. It could be giving up your job, your family, your hopes, your dreams, your future plans. Following God, most assuredly, will cost you your life. That seems a bit excessive, right? No, actually from what God's word shows us, it is pretty accurate. Let's look at a few examples.

Abram's faith cost him his home and almost cost him his only son. "Yes, but that's just one man," you might say. Then you realize that God led Moses from the comfort of living with his wife's family to leading a nation of stubborn, complaining men around in the desert for 40 years. The people of Israel, that Moses led out of Egypt and into the wilderness toward the Promised Land, left behind everything they had ever known to go to a land they had never seen. Only two men of that nation actually got to step foot into the Promised Land. Only TWO! Take a look at David, a man after God's heart. (Acts 13:22.) God anointed David as King of Israel as a young man, but David didn't spend his young adulthood sitting on a throne. Instead, he spent it hiding in caves, running for his life. When David ruled as King of Israel for a few years, his own son ran him out of town and he was back in the wilderness. Hosea, a prophet in the Old Testament, was led by God to marry a prostitute. Then Hosea's prostitute wife left him and went back to the life of prostitution. When a woman's usefulness as a prostitute was gone, it was normal, in those days, for the woman to be sold as a slave, usually for very little, to the highest bidder. Gomer's unfaithfulness to Hosea brought her to the auction block, but God wasn't finished with Hosea and Gomer. Hosea purchased unfaithful Gomer and paid full price for her. I'm certain young Hosea never could have imagined that would be God's plan for his life. You might think all of that sounds pretty extreme. Often people think that was just the way things were in the Old Testament and God was always angry. That is simply not true. Let's take a look at what the cost to follow Jesus was in the New Testament.

Levi, the tax collector, was called to follow Jesus and he left everything to follow Him. Peter, James, John, and Andrew were called to follow Jesus. Fishing was their livelihood but they dropped their nets, left their boats, left their families, their homes, everything they had to follow Him. Saul was chasing after followers of Jesus to hurt them when Jesus appeared to him and Saul (later recognized as Paul) chooses to follow Jesus completely. Paul's earthly reward for following Jesus is described in 2 Corinthians chapter 11.

> "From the Jews five times I received forty stripes minus one. Three times I was beaten with rods; once I was stoned; three times I was shipwrecked; a night and a day I have been in the deep; in journeys often, in perils of water, in perils of robbers, in perils of my own countrymen, in perils of the Gentiles, in perils in the city, in perils in the wilderness, in perils in the sea, in perils among false brethren; in weariness and toil, in sleeplessness often, in hunger and thirst, in fastings often, in cold and nakedness" (2 Corinthians 11:24-27 NKJV).

That is an exhaustive list of the cost of following Jesus in Paul's life. Historically, it is accepted that Paul was beheaded as a martyr. Peter, another of Jesus' disciples, was crucified upside down. John, the disciple Jesus loved, was boiled in oil but did not die. Since his Roman persecutors couldn't kill him, they exiled him to the island of Patmos. These examples may seem a bit extreme, but what if that is the cost of following Jesus in your life? Would you be willing to pay that high of a price?

In my personal life, following Jesus has cost me many things: friendships, jobs, income, home, comfort, sleep, convenience, space, and time to name a few things. I was just talking with my ten-year-old son today about this. He mentioned to me that following Jesus has cost him friends, community, space, and a home. I asked him if those costs were worth following Jesus. He said, "Yes." I have to agree with him. I have sacrificed. I have willingly, joyfully accepted those costs to follow Jesus so far. I will joyfully do it again.

I've heard it said, there are more Christian martyrs today than any time in the history of the world. So, to assume that following Jesus today isn't as costly as Jesus said it would be, is a gross misunderstanding of the call of Jesus. The call of Jesus—to follow Him—He said was so costly that a man will give up everything in his life. (Matthew 13:44-45.) The way through the narrow gate is hard. The cost to follow Jesus is high. The most costly things in your life are the most precious to you. Those things most precious to you must be willingly surrendered for you to follow Jesus completely. Take time right now, before continuing on, to write down the things and people where you invest your time, energy and money. This list will represent the things of value in your life. You must decide that you are willing to surrender any and all of these things, and people, if God asks you. Then you need to communicate this decision to God. This represents what could be the true cost of following Jesus in your life. He may not require it of you, but God needs to know that you are willing.

____.

____.

____.

____.

____.

____.

____.

____.

____.

CHAPTER 4
PURPOSE OF THE WILDERNESS TRAIL

The cost of following Jesus should make you think before you start your journey following Him. It is important to know the cost of the decision you are making. But once you say yes to Jesus, accepting the cost to follow Him reflects a lifestyle of worship. Accepting the cost of following Jesus declares how precious and important God is in your life. But if saying yes to following Jesus is what Jesus wants, why is the wilderness necessary?

The purpose of the wilderness is to grow holiness in you. Holiness is not as scary of a word as you might think. Leviticus 19 says, "You shall be holy, for I the Lord your God am holy" (Leviticus 19:2b). Holiness is not about specific actions. Being holy is not about dressing a certain way. It's not singing a certain style of song and it's not acting a certain way in church. The idea of holiness that we need to focus on is being separated. Not necessarily being separated *from* others, even though that may be included, but separated *to* God. Separated and set apart for a specific purpose. Set apart for God's purpose. The book of Titus tells us, "For the grace of God has appeared, bringing salvation for all people, training us to renounce ungodliness and worldly passions, and to live self-controlled, upright and godly lives in the present age" (Titus 2:11-12). There are many ways that God desires for you to be set apart. And, God desires to set you apart for some things. Following Jesus will also separate you from some things. All of this is possible in your life, but only by the grace of God. Let's examine some key areas in life that the grace of God will set you apart from, or separate you for, in your journey down the unfamiliar trail.

Separated from Egypt

Take a look back to the beginning of Exodus. Remember that the people of Israel were in slavery in Egypt. This slavery wasn't like modern servanthood, it was oppressive and harsh. The people of Israel were suffering. They were treated like property. It was a bad situation.

Exodus 2 tells us, "God heard their groaning, and God remembered his covenant with Abraham, with Isaac, and with Jacob. God saw the people of Israel- and God knew" (Exodus 2:24-25). God saw their oppression and their pain. God knew. Even if the people of Israel didn't understand, God knew and understood. God had a plan. God was going to show His mercy and grace to His people and deliver them from Egypt. God was about to set His people apart from Egypt. From Exodus chapter 3 to Exodus chapter 14, we see the plan of God to save His people from Egypt unfold. We read about God doing miracles, sending plagues, protecting His people, who couldn't protect themselves. Then there is the dialogue between Moses and Pharaoh and Moses as a mediator between God and men. Moses was God's messenger to His people, and to Pharaoh. Moses spoke to Pharaoh exactly what God told him to say, but God hardened the heart of Pharaoh so that he would not listen to God or obey His commands. And before Pharaoh actually allowed the people of Israel to leave, life got harder for the people of Israel. Listen to Moses' reaction to the people's increased hardship in Exodus chapter 5. "Why did you ever send me? For since I came to Pharaoh to speak in your name, he has done evil to this people, and you have not delivered your people at all" (Exodus 5:22b-23). Moses speaking directly to God this way shows his frustration. God has told him that

He was going to set the people of Israel free from their slavery, but Moses wasn't seeing any progress. To Moses, it was the opposite of progress. Things were getting worse for God's people. God responds, "Say therefore to my people, 'I am the Lord, and I will bring you out from under the burden of the Egyptians, and I will deliver you from slavery to them, and I will redeem you with an outstretched arm and with great acts of judgment'" (Exodus 6:6). This is a powerful statement God just made to His people, and God delivers on His promise. God delivers His people from slavery in Egypt. You may say to yourself, that's a great story about God delivering His people out of slavery, but that was a long time ago and doesn't apply to me. Can you be so sure?

You were born! You are a man or woman. You were born with a sin nature. Your very nature is sin from the beginning of your life. You were a sinner from birth and because of that, you sin and rebel against God. Look at this interaction Jesus had with descendants of Abram (Abraham). "So Jesus said to the Jews *who had believed in Him*, 'If you abide in my word, you are truly my disciples, and you will know the truth and the truth will set you free.' They answered Him, 'We are offspring of Abraham and have never been enslaved to anyone. How is it that you say, "You will become free?"' Jesus answered them, 'Truly, Truly, I say to you, everyone who practices sin is a slave to sin'" (John 8:31-34, emphasis mine). These Jews, people of Israel, had believed in Jesus. They were followers of Jesus. They were human beings (flesh) and had a sin nature. Practicing sin was a natural habit for them. Practicing sin is a natural habit for all people. Until...you encounter the truth. "You will know the truth and the truth will set you free" (John 8:32). Set you free from what? The truth sets you free from sin; it gives you an escape. Sin is deadly. "…the wages of sin is death" (Romans 6:23a). The sin nature that you and I were born with made us a slave to sin. Sin brings with it death and death is eternal separation from God. Holiness is the separation from sin *to* God. Holiness is separation *for* God's purposes and usefulness. Being a slave to sin is working in the opposite direction of holiness. Unless you get free from the slavery and nature of sin in your life, you will die and be eternally separated from God. Only the truth can set you free according to John 8:32.

In John 14 Jesus introduces you to the truth. "I am the way and THE TRUTH and the life. No one comes to the Father except through me" (John 14:6, emphasis mine). Jesus is the truth! The first step in being set apart for God is declaring Jesus as Lord of your life. This is the essence of salvation or being freed. Jesus died on the cross to take the punishment for your sins. Jesus' blood paid the price to, "forgive us our sins and to cleanse us from all unrighteousness" (1 John 1:9 NKJV). When you accept the call to follow Jesus, by God's grace, you are "a new creation; old things have passed away; behold, all things have become new" (2 Corinthians 5:17b NKJV). Over and over again in scripture salvation is referred to as being "set free." You have been set free from the bondage of sin when you choose to follow Jesus. This is the first step on the unfamiliar trail. Accepting the call of Jesus (to follow Him) is the first step in being set apart for God because you are now separated from the slavery of sin.

If you have never declared Jesus as Lord of your life and made the decision to genuinely follow Him, I encourage to make that decision right now. It's not complicated, but it is intentional. If that's you, you can pray something like this.

God, I know that I have sinned and that because of my sin, I deserve to be separated from You forever. But You sent Your son to die in my place, and He didn't stay dead, He rose from the dead. And today, God, I declare you as Lord of my life. I want to follow You and I will follow You all the days of my life. In Jesus Name, Amen.

If you prayed a prayer like that, welcome to the family of God! Next, you need to tell somebody. I encourage you to get connected to a local church and let those church leaders help you take the next steps in following Jesus.

Egypt Separated from You

God alone can separate you from the slavery of your life. It is the act of following Jesus into the wilderness (into seasons of change) that removes you from Egypt. After you have been separated from Egypt, it is important to separate Egypt from you. This seems like double work, I know, but there is a difference in the two. Let me explain. My son, Nicolas, is ten years old. He has never played basketball before on a team. He has two friends, Camden and Bradyn, who enjoy playing basketball and play on teams. When I see them play basketball together in Bradyn's driveway, I can tell by the way they dribble, pass, and shoot that Nicolas is not as experienced at playing basketball. Consider what would happen if Nicolas, completely unexperienced in basketball, was accepted onto a high school basketball team. Nicolas would be excited! He would get a jersey with a number—probably some warm-ups even, so he would look like everyone else. He would get all suited up and ready to run out with his team. Then, the team would take the court and everyone in attendance would immediately recognize—one of these things is not like the others. In an instant, any onlooker would be able to recognize that Nicolas is not ready to play high school basketball. There are several factors here. First, he is ten and not sixteen. There are some distinct differences between ten year old boys and sixteen year old boys. Besides just being younger, it would be apparent that Nicolas needs some better understanding of the game and more practice. In other words, Nicolas needs more training before he's ready for high school basketball.

Nicolas would demonstrate by his actions that he has some basketball habits that need to be changed. His shooting form is wrong. His dribbling skills are slow and broken. It would take training and time to correct these habits. Nicolas has been accepted as part of the team, but he needs to be trained in the right way.

This is the difference between separation from Egypt (salvation) and Egypt separating from you. You have been saved. You have been set free from the bondage of sin. You have been set apart from that sin nature by Jesus. You have been invited and accepted onto the team, but there is still some training needed. "For the grace of God has appeared, bringing salvation for all people, *training* us to renounce ungodliness and worldly passions" (Titus 2:11-12a, emphasis mine).

Nicolas needs to be trained in basketball to be ready to play on any team, let alone a high school basketball team. You need to be trained in holiness as you continue following God down the unfamiliar trail. Just like the people of Israel needed to be trained by God to live separate from Egypt.

Remember, Egypt was the only place any of the people of Israel had known. They had been in Egypt 430 years before God delivered them. So God, in His mercy, leads them toward the land He had promised Abram (Abraham). That Promised Land is on the other side of the wilderness. You read in Exodus chapter 12 that the people of Israel are delivered from Egypt. In Exodus chapter 14, God splits the Red Sea, the people of Israel walk across on dry ground with walls of water on either side of them, and that very same water kills all the Egyptians who were pursuing them. In Exodus chapter 16, we read about the beginning of God's provision of food for His people. In chapter 20, Moses receives the Ten Commandments on Mount Sanai. All of this is going on in the wilderness. God provided for His people's needs in the wilderness and once their basic needs were met, God began to deal with exposing the sin that still existed in their life. God had separated the people of Israel from Egypt. Now we see God beginning to separate Egypt from His people starting with the first commandment. "I am the Lord your God, who brought you out of the land of Egypt, out of the house of slavery. You shall have no other gods before me" (Exodus 20:2-3). Step one in training to renounce ungodliness, is to embrace and follow God. The New International Version of the Bible says the grace of God "teaches us to say 'No' to ungodliness" (Titus 2:12a NIV).[3]

This still speaks of training and developing certain habits.

Recently I was working with Nicolas at the basketball court. (Remember he has no basketball experience.) He was just shooting the basketball—really, it looked more like a wind-up and two handed throw at the basket. I didn't just say, "Hey Nicolas! You're doing that wrong," and wait to see what he tried next. That's not a very good trainer. I caught the basketball and walked over to him and taught him some fundamental things about shooting a basketball: bend your knees, your power comes from your legs, square up your shoulders. Your elbow on your shooting side should be under the ball. You don't push the ball at the basket, you lift with your elbow through the ball and finish with your hand down. Teaching time over. Training done. Right? Wrong. It was time to practice what he just learned; not because Nicolas is now expected to be an expert, but because it's necessary to practice doing the right thing. In order to not do the wrong thing, you do the right thing.

It is the same in your life. In order to say no to ungodliness, you have to say yes to godliness. In order to be separated from the habits of your slavery you have to continually choose freedom. You, like the people of Israel, have been delivered from slavery by God Himself. You have been given a jersey. You are on the team. But when you suit up and hit the court, it's obvious that there's still some training to do. There are still habits of your sin nature that have to be dealt with. When you accept Christ as Lord of your life, you are saved from the slavery of sin and the Holy Spirit comes to live inside of you. The Holy Spirit is the spirit of God Himself. The presence of God comes and lives inside of you. It is the picture of salvation. The picture of being justified by your faith in Christ. But, God doesn't share space. God said, "You shall have no other gods before me" (Exodus 20:3 NKJV). There is only space in your life for one Lord. Either Jesus is Lord or He is not. He does not share space. That is why, when you act like you acted before being set free from slavery to sin, God in you can't stand it. The Holy Spirit is "teaching you to say 'no' to ungodliness and worldly passion" (Titus 2:12a NIV). How you accomplish this is by saying "yes" and following Jesus. You follow Him further. You follow Jesus more closely. As you follow Jesus down the unfamiliar path for the rest of your life, He exposes sin in your life and you must deal with it. The primary way God exposes sin in your life is through His Word. That exposed sin is dealt with through repentance, or turning away from that sin. It is through this process that you are "conformed to the image of His Son (Christ)" (Romans 8:29). Through this process your life looks more like the life of Christ and less like your life in slavery to sin. Your Egypt, or sin nature, is being separated from you. It is a lifelong process called sanctification. When you see or hear the word sanctification, just imagine being molded and shaped by the Holy Spirit into the image of Jesus. It is God separating Egypt from you.

Hearing from God

In the two years we lived in Colorado, my family and I were privileged to attend Radiant Church—a great community of believers. In 2014, Pastor Todd Hudnall preached a series on the tabernacle entitled, "God's Mobile Home."[4] It was a great look at God's design of the tabernacle and why it is so important for us today. You can find the series at www.radiantchurch.org. One particular sermon that has stayed with me in the series is the "The Brazen Laver," from July 13th, 2014. If you were going to enter the tabernacle, you had to come through the East Gate. It was the only way into the tabernacle, just as Jesus is the only way to the Father. Once you walked through the East Gate you come into the Outer Court and the first fixture you encounter is the brazen, or bronze, altar. This is the altar of sacrifice. According to God's law (Leviticus 17:11), "without the shedding of blood there is no forgiveness of sins" (Hebrews 9:22). There had to be a blood sacrifice for our sins to be forgiven; and in the Old Testament, the practice was for the sacrifice of the blood of a lamb to take your place. It was always acceptable for one to die in the place of another. Jesus was our spotless lamb who gave His life for our sins and His blood that was shed on the cross paid for our sins to be forgiven. Jesus fulfilled the requirements of the brazen altar. Praise God for the completed work of Jesus on the cross of Calvary!

However, even though you were at the brazen altar, you were not yet in the presence of God. The next place you came to was the brazen laver, or basin. You read about it in Exodus chapter 30. The brazen laver was a washing station. This washing station was for the priests to wash their hands and feet after they had made sacrifices. God told Moses, "When they go into the tent of meeting, or when they come near the altar to minister, to burn a food offering to the Lord, they shall wash with water, so that they may not die" (Exodus 30:20). God's desire was for His priests to be clean and pure. God's desire was for those doing ministry to be clean. They washed all the time. My practice would have been, when in doubt wash it out. If there was any doubt in my mind whether I needed to wash or not, I would wash my hands and feet. Why? It's better than the alternative—Death! The regular washing at the laver was a type of sanctification. It was a regular cleansing of the hands and feet of the priests. Their hands represented the purifying of their actions. Their feet represented the purifying of where they went or the direction of their life. We all need purification in our lives continually. One of the most intriguing attributes of the brazen laver is the fact that it was made of polished bronze or copper. Similar to the mirrors that the women would use in those days—this polished bronze (or copper) would allow you to see yourself as you were washing. This is vital in understanding our need for continual purification. If you can't see the mess on your hands, how can you know that your hands are clean? If you can't see an honest reflection of who you are, your own actions and the direction of your life, then you will never be able to make necessary changes. This reflection and clear view of who you are primarily comes from God's Word. Scripture gives us a clearer picture of who we are in comparison to who God is. God's Word and following God's voice is vital for purifying your life. Hearing God's voice clearly is absolutely necessary for the work of holiness in your life.

God's Word, the Bible, is God's voice. "All scripture is breathed out by God and profitable for teaching, for reproof, for correction, and for training in righteousness, that the man of God may be complete, equipped for every good work" (2 Timothy 3:16-17). The Bible is God actively speaking to you, even today. Right now. God is speaking to you through His word. God is teaching you through His word. The Holy

Spirit is correcting you through His word. When you take an honest look into God's word, it will expose places in your life that need to be cleaned up. It allows you to see things in yourself that you would not have seen otherwise. The voice of God convicts and corrects the anger that lashes out when we don't like what we see or hear. God's Word teaches us that instead of fits of anger, we can have peace, patience, and kindness through the Holy Spirit. This can happen even on the unfamiliar trail of our life following Christ.

God leads us into the wilderness for us to hear His voice clearly. "I will allure her, and bring her into the wilderness, and speak tenderly to her" (Hosea 2:14). God doesn't compete with the noise of your life. God doesn't yell at you to get your attention. If you are listening to Him, He is typically speaking softly, gently. According to Hosea, He often leads you into the wilderness to speak to you this way. That doesn't mean that you have to be in a wilderness in your life to hear God's voice, but it is much simpler because we are looking and listening to find our way. You know where the people of Israel were when the brazen laver was communicated, built and commissioned? You guessed it, the wilderness. You may not realize that for almost 400 years, from the time Joseph died at the end of Genesis to the beginning of Exodus when Moses is born, there is no mention of hearing God's voice. Then God speaks to Moses at Horeb on the back side of the desert. (Exodus 3) For forty years (which is contained in 4 books of the Bible) God speaks to His people regularly, all while they are in the wilderness. God lead His people into the wilderness to speak to them and show them that they were in need of His Word. This was intentional for God to establish the value of what Jesus would quote when He was in the wilderness and being tempted. "Man shall not live by bread alone, but by every word that comes from the mouth of God" (Matthew 4:4). You don't live just on food and water, you need God's Word alive and active in your life. You need to make space for God's Word in your life. God's Word is life-giving. Read God's Word. Study God's Word. Know God's Word. Follow God's Word. I thought I was supposed to follow Jesus? Yes. John 1:1-2 says, "In the beginning was the Word, and the Word was with God, and the Word was God. He (meaning Jesus) was in the beginning with God" (John 1:1-2, emphasis mine). John chapter 1 goes on to say, "And the Word became flesh and dwelt among us" (John 1:14). Jesus is the Word. If you are going to accept the call to follow Jesus, He will lead you down the unfamiliar trail and into the wilderness. He is going before you and, if you are His, you will know His voice. (John 10:4) You will know His voice and it will give life to you. The wilderness is an important place to hear the voice of God and get to know the heart of

God.

Knowing God More

About 4,000 years ago, it was common to see cultures represent their gods in the image of familiar things. In Egypt especially, it was common for their many gods and goddesses to be represented by animals. Their many gods were impersonal and distant.[5] The Egyptians believed they had to earn the gods' favor through sacrifices and rituals. Their gods represented some different powers of nature, such as: the moon, the sun, the wind, and even death. In the Egyptians understanding, these gods were separated from them and their sacrifices and rituals were to please the gods. They didn't just pray to their gods. The Egyptians' religious practices would have included: divination, oracles, magic, and contact with the dead. This is the culture where the people of Israel were grown—from a small family to a great nation, from 12 brothers to hundreds of thousands of men (plus women and children)—over a period of 430 years. God saw His people and knew their need.

God knew His people needed to be free from the slavery of Egypt. He knew the need to distance the people of Israel from Egypt so He could free His people from the lifestyle of Egypt. God's desire was for His people to hear

His voice and for them to know Him. God was going to completely change the life of His people. He was setting His people apart from other people. He was separating His people not only in the words they would use, but in the way they would live, the way they would worship, and the God they would serve and know. This made God's people an unusual group. A peculiar people.

The people of Israel, when they were led out of Egypt, didn't have a home land. They weren't the nation of Israel because, in reality, they didn't have a nation. They didn't have borders that they lived in. They didn't even have houses. They lived in tents because everything they owned had to be able to move when God moved. Think about that for a minute. They roamed around in the wilderness, following a cloud during the day and fire at night, completely exposed for forty years. They had no walls to hide behind. They had no wells that they had dug to provide water. They had no vineyards or orchards planted to provide fruit or drink. They didn't plant any fields, or gather any grain to make bread or any other foods to eat. But the people of Israel, and their animals, never went without food or drink. God was showing Himself to be different than the gods of all the other people in the area. God was showing His people that He wasn't distant and unknowable, or disinterested in their lives. God chose His people and delivered them from slavery in

Egypt because He loved them. "I am the Lord your God, who brought you out of the land of Egypt, out of the house of slavery. You shall have no other gods before me" (Exodus 20:2-3). In fact, God didn't just set His people free from Egypt, He began to remove the habits of Egypt from their lives, and began to speak to them by giving them some rules to live by. God also invited His people into a relationship with Him.

This would seem really strange and probably a little awkward to someone who had learned their entire life that gods are impersonal. This would be where the people of Israel found themselves. You can begin to understand why the people of Israel were afraid of God. "Now when all the people saw the thunder and the flashes of lightning and the sound of the trumpet and the mountain smoking, the people were afraid and trembled, and stood far off and said to Moses, 'You speak to us, and we will listen; but do not let God speak to us, lest we die'" (Exodus 20:18-19). In their experience, when disaster came it was the judgment of one of the gods. A god that was not benevolent, or concerned with them, but one that was acting however it wanted to act. Why? Because it could. That was not, and is not, the nature of the Lord God, but they didn't know that. The people of Israel had not learned that yet. God, through much of 21 chapters (Exodus 20-40), teaches the people of Israel His laws, instructing them how to build the tabernacle, and empowering them to build it. God spent all that time telling His people He wanted to know them, and God wanted the people of Israel to know Him. He instructed them on how to deal with each other. He gave them instructions on how to come before Him. God taught them about resting on the Sabbath day and honoring Him with feasts to remember what He had done for His people. God did not spare details. God wanted His people to know that He had come to them. And when the tabernacle was finished, God showed His people that He had not only come to them, but God had provided a way for His people to come to Him and know Him. God, the creator of heaven and earth and everything on the earth, rested the glory of His presence in the middle of His people. "Then the cloud covered the tent of meeting, and the glory of the Lord filled the tabernacle" (Exodus 40:34). "For the cloud of the Lord was on the tabernacle by day, and fire was in it by night, in the sight of all the house of Israel throughout all their journeys" (Exodus 40:38). God showed the people of Israel that He was available to them and wanted a more intimate relationship with them "throughout all their journeys" (Exodus 40:38b). Great news for the people of Israel, but I was not born a Jew. What about you? So where do you and I come into this story?

Over the next 1500 years or so, God's people serve

Him and forget Him, remember Him and neglect Him, obey His law and compromise His teaching—over and over and over again. The people of Israel find it impossible to actually live up to the requirements of the law of God. God didn't stop communicating with His people for almost 1100 years through all their rebellions, sinfulness, and rebuilding. He sent prophet upon prophet to guide them. Then God kept silent for about 400 years. God broke His silence through a virgin giving birth to God's son, the promised Messiah, in a stable. In Isaiah chapter 49, God says, "I am the Lord your SAVIOR, and your redeemer, the Mighty One of Jacob" (Isaiah 49:26b, emphasis mine). God declared He is your savior. Then Jesus is born! "And in the same region there were shepherds out in the field, keeping watch over their flock by night. And an angel of the Lord appeared to them, and the glory of the Lord shone around them, and they were filled with great fear. And the angel said to them, 'Fear not, for behold, I bring you good news of great joy that will be *for all the people.* For unto you is born this day in the city of David a SAVIOR, who is Christ the Lord" (Luke 2:8-11, emphasis mine). God just declared, through His angel, that Jesus was the Savior. The long-awaited Messiah was here. If you look back at that passage, the angel didn't say this news was for God's people or for Israel but "for all the people." God loved you so much that He wouldn't send His son just for a certain people but "for all the people." That includes you! That includes me!

Jesus came to be your Savior! Jesus came to set you free from the slavery of sin, just like God did for the children of Israel. God set the people of Israel apart to Himself and made them a peculiar people because they didn't live like everyone else around them. Israel did not worship or serve many gods: Israel served the Lord God. Israel did not choose God: God chose Israel to be His people. God chose that generation of the people of Israel to witness His glory and to experience His deliverance. Israel was chosen. God made Israel a nation. God made Israel peculiar. Jesus has done the same for you. Jesus chose to show mercy and grace to you. Jesus has made you set apart, or holy. Jesus is still separating you from sin. If you follow Jesus down the unfamiliar trail, He will continue to make you seem peculiar to this world. "But ye (you) are a chosen generation, a royal priesthood, an holy nation, a peculiar people" (1 Peter 2:9a KJV).[6] Jesus paid the price to set you free from your slavery to sin on the cross. Jesus conquered death—the consequences of your sin—in your life through His resurrection. Jesus continues to speak to you, and invites you to know Him more closely, by leaving this earth and sending His Spirit to live inside of you.

When you choose to follow Jesus down the unfamiliar

trail and into the wilderness, your life may seem peculiar to others. You will never be the same again.

CHAPTER 5
THE FAR SIDE OF THE WILDERNESS

The people of Israel have been delivered from Egypt for many years. God has lead them all around this wilderness. They have built the tabernacle as God instructed them. They have won battles. They ate manna for food. They were in relationship with God. Where God led, His people went. When His glory cloud stopped, they set up camp. The people of Israel lived life trusting God for everything and following Him every day. You would think at this point God would just lead them right into the land of Promise. But God, their loving Father, had their best interest in mind on the back side of the wilderness.

Reminded of the Covenant

"In the fortieth year, on the first day of the eleventh month, Moses spoke to the people of Israel according to all that the Lord had given him in commandment to them" (Deuteronomy 1:3). Forty years the people had followed God. Forty years they had trusted God, been corrected by God, been sustained by God. Forty years! All but a few of the men of age (who left Egypt) were even still alive. God had changed what was considered normal for an entire generation. The people of Israel that were standing in front of Moses forty years later were much different than the ones who had feared for their lives at the edge of the Red Sea. They had so much experience at trusting and following God. How much more instruction could they possibly need? Evidently they needed a little more. God Almighty knew their hearts. He knew them intimately. From "the first month in the second year, on the first day of the month" (Exodus 40:17), God had invited them into His presence. For 38 years of their lives, they had known God: not known about Him, but had known Him. He was their God and they were His people. No question about it. But still, at the far side of the wilderness, God spent a little extra time reminding His people of His commitment to them and their commitment to Him. Why take the time to go back over what they had just experienced? Why take the time to remind them of what they had chronicled the entire time in the wilderness? They had the evidence of what God had done all around them. This seems completely unnecessary, but God saw His people and knew.

Faithfulness—that's the reason to retell the story. God intended for His people to remember His faithfulness. God needed them to recognize the reason they were standing where they were—because God made it possible. God spent time reminding them that He brought them out of Egypt, that He organized them. (Numbers 2.) God supplied for their appetite. (Exodus 16.) God made the bitter water drinkable. (Exodus 15.) Over and over and over again, God had done what the people were not able to do for themselves. God was reminding His people of His faithfulness to them. God wanted His people to recognize that the reason they were there was because of their faithfulness to Him. You cannot tell the story of the wilderness without dealing with the fact that unfaithfulness to God, in the wilderness, had been fatal…more than once. The previous generation didn't see the Promised Land because of their rebellion (or unfaithfulness). "And I (Moses) said to you, 'you have come to the hill country of the Amorites, which the Lord our God is giving us. See, the Lord your God has set the land before you. Go up, take possession, as the Lord, the God of your fathers, has told you'" (Deuteronomy 1:20-21, clarification mine). "Yet you would not go up, but rebelled against the command of the Lord your God" (Deuteronomy 1:26). "And the Lord heard your words and was angered, and He swore, 'Not one of these men of this evil generation shall see the good land that I swore to give to your fathers'" (Deuteronomy 1:34-35). Remember, that generation is already dead! The people Moses is talking to are not the ones who chose to rebel against God in this way. This happened so long ago. They were different people now. But were they? God was going through the entire story in detail to show them the rebellion of their lives apart from Him. He contrasted this throughout the story with how His provision and protection was overwhelming when they were living in faithful obedience to His voice. Yes, they had experienced all the things Moses told them. Yes, they had the tabernacle as a reminder. But so often in life, we take for granted the things that God has already done and has already said to us. It is easy to get so comfortable with hearing God's voice that we are always wanting something "new" and "fresh".

It's like a girl opening presents at her birthday party. So many friends and family members have come to celebrate her birthday. There are games and fun. Everyone eats cake and ice cream. Then someone mentions that it's time to open presents. All the kids get seated to watch and a chair is pulled up for the birthday girl next to this mountain of presents. The picture takers make sure they are all in place. There's no rule on which present to open first, so one is drawn from the pile at random. They read who the gift is from and the birthday girl opens the gift. She is genuinely excited about what she got and shows the gift off to everyone. Picture takers get their photo for memory's sake and the process is repeated for all of the presents. Put yourself in that little girl's chair. When you are opening gift number 28, do you even remember what gift number 4 was, or are you just going through the motions? You tell everyone "thank you" because you are genuinely thankful, but you don't really understand what all you have received. Eventually the party is over, everything has been cleaned up, and everyone is gone. That is when you get a more clear understanding of what you have been given. That's very similar to what God is doing in the retelling of the story in Deuteronomy. God's people had seen all kinds of miraculous things happen. But God had given them so much, it was almost impossible to have remembered all of it at the time. God's people needed to be reminded of the process they had gone through. The people of Israel needed to be reminded to stay committed to the covenant God had given them. And when you find yourself on the back side of the wilderness, following the unfamiliar path, don't be surprised when God reminds you of what He's already taught you.

Read Paul's writings to the churches. Many of Paul's letters dealt with specific areas of concern in that particular church. Yet in every letter, he clearly communicates the truth of Jesus as the only way to salvation. In 1 Corinthians chapter 1, Paul writes, "I give thanks to my God always for you because of the grace of God that was given you in Jesus Christ" (1 Corinthians 1:4). In Galatians, "we know that a person is not justified by works of the law but through faith in Jesus Christ" (Galatians 2:16a). In Ephesians, "now in Christ Jesus you who once were far off have been brought near by the blood of Christ" (Ephesians 2:13). Paul is writing to the churches. These are people who have said yes to following Jesus. They knew the truth of Christ. They knew the cost of following Jesus. They knew because Paul himself had taught them, and he always left a trained disciple behind to train up other disciples. Paul reminded them, not because they didn't know, but because they needed to be reminded of the work of Christ and its completeness: so they would not depart from it or add to it. You are the same way. Don't be surprised when you find yourself on the far side of the wilderness and God reminds you of what He has already done. Don't be surprised when you get to that point and hear God tell you what He's already told you. His reminders are for your good, so that you don't forget that it is because of Jesus that you have found your way to where you are—and it is going to be Jesus who leads you on. God is reminding you to keep your eyes focused on Christ.

Focus on God

In the movie, *Rise of the Guardians*[7], you see a familiar scene. Jack Frost, the newly chosen guardian, is struggling with who he is and why the Man in the Moon chose him as a guardian. Jack is shown his past. Jack finds himself reliving a memory of his family from many years ago. He was going to play on the ice with his sister. Jack's sister goes out on the ice first and finds herself in a spot where the ice is not strong enough to hold her. Jack says, "It's ok, it's ok. Don't look down. Just look at me."

"Jack, I'm scared," she replies as she looks down and the ice continues to crack.

"I know. I know," Jack responds. Jack tries to step closer to his sister, as the ice starts to crack under his feet as well. "But you're gonna be alright. You're not gonna fall in. Uh." Jack is looking around to think and an idea comes to him. "We're gonna have a little fun instead."

"No, we're not!" Jack's sister exclaims.

"Would I trick you?"

"Yes, you always play tricks!" She replies frantically.

"Well...Alright...Well," Jack chuckles, "not, not, not this time. I promise. I promise, you're gonna be...gonna be fine." Jack says calmingly. "You have to believe in me." Everyone begins to breathe deeper, as if a calm has come in the middle of their panic. "You wanna play a game?" Jack asked. "We're gonna play hop scotch. Like we play every day. It's as easy as, uh, one!" Jack steps to the right. The ice cracks under his foot. Jack puts all his weight on that foot and balances himself. "Whoa!" Jack exclaimed, while waving his arms and smiling, all while still balancing on his right leg. "Two!" Jack takes another few steps to his right. He finds safety on solid ice just a few feet away.

"Three!" He picks up his staff of sorts, similar to a shepherds staff. "Alright. Now it's your turn." He kneels down on the ice, beginning to reach toward his sister with the staff. "One!" His sister begins to wobble toward him on her ice skates and the ice continues to weaken under her. "That's it, that's it! Two!" She continues to inch closer to Jack, becoming more concerned she will fall in. "Three!" At that moment, Jack reaches out his staff, grabs his sister with the hook at the end and slings her to safety across the ice. Jack has saved his little sister.

Jack Frost is just a fictional character in a made up story, but this is a common scene that many movies have portrayed. A child, or bystander, finds themselves in harm's way, either through the actions of a villain or through natural events. They are in danger. Many times, they are literally hanging on for their life. The hero will tell them, "look at me." Why would the hero do that? I believe, most often, the hero's purpose is to calm the victim, giving the victim something to focus on in the moment. The hero is trying to remove their fear of death, and to replace it with intentional action.

You have faithfully, obediently followed Jesus to this point. It has been costly in many ways. The journey has been challenging and, in some instances, painful, but that's part of the process of being separated from sin. The joy of the Lord, and the freedom that you now walk in, makes all that you have endured, worth it. You aren't just obedient in following Christ, you follow with pleasure. God has blessed you with more than you need. You have been able to give to others. You have been able to share your story with others and see them choose to follow Jesus down the unfamiliar trail. Then something happens that is completely out of your control. Your car breaks down. Your boss informs you that the company is struggling and they are going to have to cut your job. Someone in your family, possibly you, starts having health issues out of nowhere. You get the report—it's cancer and it's aggressive. These can be devastating to anyone. Just ask Job.

"There was a man in the land of Uz whose name was Job, and that man was blameless and upright, one who feared God and turned away from evil" (Job 1:1). Job followed and trusted God. Job followed God close enough that God mentioned Job to Satan. "And the Lord said to Satan, "Have you considered my servant Job, that there is none like him on the earth, a blameless and upright man, who fears God and turns away from evil" (Job 1:8)? Job was recognized by God for being committed to Him. According to God's account of Job, wouldn't you say he was unusual compared to other people? If there is none like him, that would make him different from other people. Then one day, Sabeans took all 1,000 of Job's oxen and 500 donkeys and killed all the servants who were looking after them, except one. Fire fell from heaven and consumed the 7,000 sheep and the servants watching the sheep, except one. Chaldeans took all 3,000 of his camels and killed all the servants who looked after the camels, except one. A mighty wind came across the wilderness and hit the house of his oldest son and it fell down, killing all of Job's seven sons and three daughters. (Job 1:13-19.) Now that was a tough day! Nothing that happened to Job on that day was in Job's control. Job was unusual. Job was set apart by God. Job was following God down the unfamiliar path, even though he never left home.

God had established him. God had provided for him. God had made Job "the greatest of all the people of the east" (Job 1:3b). And now God allowed all that Job had gained over a lifetime of trusting and serving God to be taken in a day. One day, a literal 24 hour period of time. God was proving a point to Satan through Job. Proving that Job's focus was God and not the things God had given him. Job proved God to be true by his reaction. "Then Job arose and tore his robe and shaved his head and fell on the ground and worshiped. And he said, 'Naked I came from my mother's womb, and naked shall I return. The Lord gave and the Lord has taken away; blessed be the name of the Lord'" (Job 1:20-21). Job experienced what has to be one of the worst, if not the worst, days ever recorded in human history. I promise you I have never experienced a day like that day for Job. I'm guessing you haven't experienced a day like that either. You've had tough days. You've probably even experienced days of great loss. Most people probably haven't lost every possession and family member in one day. Job was distraught. Job was heartbroken. Job was mourning. That's why he tore his robe and shaved his head. But he did something that is not in human nature. Job fell to the ground and worshiped God. That's not normal. That's not usual. Job didn't look at all the terrible things going on around him and freeze in fear. Job focused on God. He acknowledged that God gave him what he had and that God could take it away. Even though I have never experienced a day anywhere near that bad, I can't say with certainty that I would have responded the way Job did. What about you?

God had led the people of Israel throughout the wilderness. He brought them to the far side of the wilderness. Forty years after they had been delivered from Egypt, God was taking the time to make sure the people of Israel were focused on Him. God knew what Israel did not. When they crossed over into the Promised Land, the pillar of cloud and fire would be gone. The manna was going to stop. God was delivering them to the Promised Land. God stopped the people before they entered the Promised Land to remind them to focus their life on following and trusting Him. No matter how the physical world seemed, God was to be the focus. In famine and plenty, God was to be the focus. In harvest time and planting time, God was to be the focus. God's desire for you is the same.

Your covenant with God (your vow to Him) includes: that in sickness and in health, for richer or for poorer, you will follow Him. No matter what happens in your life, God will be the focus. Even if you have a day like Job, you can have the emotions—frustration, heartbreak, and mourning—without losing focus on God. On the far side of the wilderness, God will remind you to keep your heart and life focused on Him because opposition is coming.

Greater Resistance

God led the hundreds of thousands of people of Israel throughout the wilderness for forty years. They didn't just aimlessly wander; they were purposed by God in the way that they should go. God took them to Mount Sanai and, before giving His people the Ten Commandments, gave them a promise. "If you will indeed obey my voice and keep my covenant, then you shall be a special treasure to me above all people; for all the earth is mine. And you shall be to me a kingdom of priests and a holy nation" (Exodus 19:5-6 NKJV). God made this commitment to His people just three months after they left Egypt and before the Ten Commandments. God was committed to His people being set apart and in relationship with Him. God committed to speaking to His people because, without hearing His voice, the people of Israel could not obey His voice. God continually tells the people of Israel that He would "bring you into the land which I swore to give to Abraham, Isaac, and Jacob" (Exodus 6:8a NKJV). For context, look back at the call of Abraham (Abram) in Genesis chapter 12. God tells Abram go "to a land I will show you. I will make you a great nation; I will bless you and make your name great; and you shall be a blessing. I will bless those who bless you, and I will curse those who curse you" (Genesis 12:1b-3 NKJV). This is the original call of Abram. The true covenant was in Genesis chapter 15. "On that day the Lord made a covenant with Abram, saying, 'To your offspring I give this land, the river of Egypt to the great river, the river Euphrates" (Genesis 15:18). God promised this land to Abraham and his offspring: which included every person of Israel in the wilderness. God was going to fulfill His promise to His people. One thing I think is peculiar, in God's call of Abram in Genesis 12, is the line "I will curse those who curse you" (Exodus 12:3b NKJV). God implies that there will be people who oppose Abraham and his offspring. It didn't take the people of Israel much time in the wilderness to find this to be true.

Exodus chapter 17 tells of one such account. "Then Amalek came and fought with Israel at Rephidim" (Exodus 17:8). Amalek came out to oppose the people of Israel because he felt threatened by God's people. He had never seen any people like these. Normally, nomadic people were a small group of travelers, not a nation of this size. It would not be unusual to assume a group of men of that size was an army—a very strong army—except that there were women and children everywhere. The people of God wandering in the wilderness were an imposing sight. If every one of the

603,550 men counted in Numbers Chapter 2 had a tent that was ten feet long by ten feet wide, (100 sq. ft.) then the minimum amount of land needed for the people of Israel to make camp was 2.165 square miles. And that total land area would not include any personal space, the tabernacle, or the tribe of Levi. Imagine that size! They were a huge camp of people. An imposing sight to any established city or people. Amalek had to feel that way. Not only that, but remember they have no fortress to run to, no fortification to hide behind for rest, or a break in fighting to regain strength. The people of Israel are completely exposed to attack.

God had placed His people in this position intentionally. God's people, wandering in the wilderness without a stronghold, without a city of refuge, had only two possible outcomes to a serious battle. The people of Israel would either completely destroy their enemy, or they would be destroyed by their enemy. Any other outcome would not make sense. If Israel left any enemy survivors to rebuild, they would surely have to fight with them again at a later time. If Israel wasn't completely destroyed by this enemy, they would be extremely vulnerable to the next attack. God led the people of Israel in the wilderness and made it absolutely vital for their continued existence as a nation for them to know, before they fought, that God was leading them into battle. God was with them in the fight against Amalek. "So Moses said to Joshua, 'Choose for us men, and go out and fight with Amalek. Tomorrow I will stand on the top of the hill with the staff of God in my hand.' Whenever Moses held up his hand, Israel prevailed, and whenever he lowered his hand Amalek prevailed. And Joshua overwhelmed Amalek and his people with the sword" (Exodus 17:9, 11, 13). The staff of God being lifted up was the victory in the fight with Amalek. When God led the fight, the victory was already secure. When you find yourself in a fight that God has led you to, lift up the name of the Lord, for He has already won the battle.

You will be opposed in your life. You will find opposition if you are following Jesus. "I have said all these things to you, that in me you may have peace. In the world you WILL HAVE TRIBULATION. But take heart; I HAVE OVERCOME THE WORLD" (John 16:33, emphasis mine). Jesus told you that you would be opposed in this life. Your life here on the earth will have troubles. Some troubles in your life are natural obstacles but, if you follow Jesus down the unfamiliar trail, there will be greater and greater resistance. Jesus said you would have tribulations, opposition, and resistance in this life, but He said don't worry. The Amplified Bible says, "be of good cheer [take courage, be confident, certain, undaunted]" (John 16:33 AMP)![8] All of these interpretations of the word are accurate. Have courage, cheer, confidence, and certainty that JESUS has already won the battle. Jesus has already overcome the fight that you are in, so join him in the fight. You are fighting on the side of the creator of the universe. Don't be afraid of the fight; jump into it with everything you've got. God has already taken care of everything that you need and brought you to the far side of the wilderness. You will have greater resistance in your life because you are following Jesus. Jesus has led you into the wilderness and away from any other place that you could use as a stronghold, or fortress, except him. So you have a choice to make. Will you see the opposition and fight with Jesus against the enemy, or will you run for your life and desert him?

You have to choose to fight for Jesus. When you follow Jesus, you will have to learn to fight spiritually. Ephesians tells us, "Finally, be strong in the Lord and in the strength of your might. Put on the whole armor of God, that you may be able to stand against the schemes of the devil" (Ephesians 6:10-11). You must be prepared to fight against the schemes of Satan. Some of those attacks will come from places you least expect. "I have said all these things to you to keep you from falling away. They will put you out of the synagogues. Indeed, the hour is coming when whoever kills you will think he is offering service to God" (John 16:1-2). Jesus was telling His disciples that, when they felt resistance and pressure from religious leaders, they should not back down. He was encouraging them not to compromise the truth of the Word. Jesus was telling His disciples to trust Him more than anything else—even religious leaders. You may think this is a strange instruction from Jesus, but just take a look at church history. Most of the New Testament books written by Paul were letters of correction to the churches and church leaders of the first century church. (Keep in mind that Paul dies about 30 years after Jesus.)

Look forward to the 16th century and a man by the name of Martin Luther[9]. Martin Luther lead the Protestant movement by defying the stance of the Roman Catholic Church which said that only the Pope could interpret scripture. He nailed his (now famous) 95 theses to the door of a Catholic chapel in 1517 A.D. Martin Luther was not motivated by selfishness or greed or fame. He was motivated by God showing himself to be real in his life. Martin Luther was excommunicated from the Roman Catholic Church in 1521 A.D. Later in 1521, he was declared a heretic—a person teaching a doctrine opposed by the Roman Catholic Church. Because Martin Luther refused to back down from the truth of God in scripture, and his 95 theses were not opposed to the truth of God's Word, he found himself in the wilderness and is credited today with beginning the Protestant Church, the church that empowered the understanding of scripture and right of priesthood to every believer. This is a truth from Exodus chapter 19 and 1 Peter chapter 2, that was echoed by Martin Luther.

It is absolutely necessary for you, as a follower of Jesus, to know Him intimately, to know and follow the teaching of God's Word, and hear to Jesus' voice lead you. Otherwise, when the day comes that you face opposition, you will allow doubt and fear to lead you instead of Christ.

Refuse to Settle

My family and I started a workout routine after Christmas last year. We have been doing some plyometric and cardio workouts three days a week. If those terms are completely foreign to you, as they were to me a short time ago, let me offer some clarity. The first week we started with three sets of eight repetitions of box jumps, squat jumps, lateral jumps and power skips for our plyometric workout time. Each of us, the kids included, would jog at our own pace for 5 minutes. That was our workout. Having not worked out consistently over our 11 years of marriage and having a tendency to drink soda instead of water, I was really sore after the first two workouts—REALLY sore. I was stiff and frustrated that my body didn't bounce back the way it always had before. By the end of the week, the soreness was going away and I recognized that I had more stamina and strength throughout the workout. Progress! Everyone's bodies seemed to handle the workout better. The next week, we had a choice to make—would we say that working out as a family for a week was good enough? Would we decide to keep working out the same way or would we keep working out and push ourselves a little more?

If we gave up after one week, we would always be able to say we tried working out as a family but it just didn't work out for us. If we continued working out, doing the same workout routine, we could be certain (and possibly content) with the fact that we were more active than many other families. If we kept working out and challenging ourselves, refusing to settle, we might find ourselves in some uncomfortable positions and have some physical pain in the process. But, we would know that we could do challenging things—that a few weeks ago were beyond our capability—and continue to push forward. These ideas represent some distinct thought processes in the church today.

I have had many conversations with people who say they went to church as a kid; they tried the whole "Christian thing" but it just didn't work for them. They will go on to justify their stance by listing off all the problems they endured at the church, much like I could have given up on working out after the first week and said it didn't work out for me. I would justify it by all the parts of my body that experienced pain. What I would be telling you is that the reward of working out is not worth the hardship to me. Essentially, people who say they have tried Christ and He didn't work for them, are telling me they really didn't get to know Jesus. They decided the hardship of dealing with people who are in the same process of becoming free from their sin is not worth the reward of following Jesus. They chose to settle for death instead of life. They have chosen to be separated from God forever. They have fallen away. (John 16:1.)

Still, there are others who justify their "good position." Some people have followed Jesus faithfully down the unfamiliar path and find a spot to settle. These people have chosen what seems acceptable and good in their own eyes and decide that it is "good enough." This is not a new thing. In Numbers chapter 32 you read about the tribes of Gad, Reuben, and half the tribe of Manasseh having a great multitude of livestock. They see "the land of Jazer and the land of Gilead, and behold, the place was a place for livestock" (Numbers 32:1b). These tribes come before Moses and the elders and asked for a favor. They beg really. They said, "Let this land be given to your servants as a possession. Do not take us over the Jordan" (Numbers 32:5 NKJV). Did you hear what they said? Do not take us over the Jordan!

They just came before Moses and the elders and basically said, "We know that God's Promised Land is on the other side of the Jordan but this land right here is good for our livestock." They willingly chose a place in the wilderness and decided it was good enough. Moses makes a deal with them. The deal was this: as long as their men of war went over the Jordan to fight for the Land of Promise, they could have the land they wanted. God didn't respond with such a kind offer. "And the Lord's anger was kindled on that day, and he swore, saying, 'Surely none of the men who came up out of Egypt, from twenty years old and upward, shall see the land that I swore to give to Abraham, to Isaac, and to Jacob, because they have not wholly followed me, none except Caleb the son of Jephunneh the Kenizzite and Joshua the son of Nun, for they have wholly followed the Lord'" (Numbers 32:10-12). The people of Gad, Reuben, and half the tribe of Manasseh, choosing to settle for less than what God was leading them to, cost every man over 20 years old who came out of Egypt the promise of God. Seems a little drastic maybe, but the people chose to settle for less than following God completely. It turned out to be a very costly choice.

The choice of settling for less than total dependence on Jesus is a costly one. The choice to justify yourself by comparing your obedience and holiness to others will never be good enough to God. Jesus did not call you to do more than the person who lives across the street. Jesus didn't call His disciples to be better followers than almost everybody else. You see, followers either follow or they don't. People don't mostly follow or follow a little bit. You are either following Jesus completely or you are not following Him at all. There is no following from a distance. Once the person you are following "from a distance" goes beyond your sight, you are no longer following, but only guessing where they went. Jesus didn't call you to "follow Him" and really mean "let's play hide and seek." Jesus called you by name, led you onto the narrow, unfamiliar path, and said, "Follow me." That means follow until the end.

You can go further than you think you can. You can follow Jesus closer than you think you can. You just have to trust Him. If you will look back and remember where you were and where God has brought you to, it will give you the courage and trust necessary to follow Jesus further. That is what God's Word says in Revelation chapter 12. "They have conquered him (Satan) by the blood of the Lamb (Jesus) and the word of their testimony, for they loved not their lives even unto death" (Revelation 12:11, clarification mine). You will overcome the difficulty of your life on the unfamiliar trail (in the wilderness) through the sacrifice that Jesus already made: by remembering and speaking about your own experiences following Jesus, by remembering how God's word has proven to be true, and by talking about how Jesus has changed your life, changed your heart, and set you free from self-destruction. Be reminded today of how good God has been in your life. Be encouraged through your own story of God's faithfulness. Recognize that you have more spiritual strength and stamina than you did when you first started following Jesus, and follow Him a little further. The reward of eternal life in the presence of God, and leading others toward the same future, is worth every pain and discomfort in this life.

Only you can make the choice to continue following Jesus beyond the far side of the wilderness. Only you can choose to allow all that God desires to do in your life to be done. Will you choose to follow Jesus through all the discomfort and pain of life on the unfamiliar trail? Will you choose not to settle for a "good enough" Christian life? Only you can decide if the pain is worth the reward.

CHAPTER 6
DEPENDENCE

Sheep are intriguing creatures. One of the most recognized traits of sheep, and their behavior, is that they flock or follow. Sheep, even very young sheep, naturally follow the older members of the flock. It is an amazing trait. The flocking and following instinct of sheep is so strong that it caused the death of 400 sheep in eastern Turkey back in 2006. The sheep plunged to their death after one of the sheep tried to cross a 15-meter deep ravine, and the rest of the flock followed. Sheep are followers. They are born to follow. Sheep flock primarily as protective instinct against predators. Their flocking and following instincts make sheep very easy to herd. Sheep were one of the earliest animals to be domesticated, and they have been thoroughly domesticated. It is doubtful they could survive in the wild, if a predator risk existed.[10]

I don't consider myself an expert on sheep or shepherding. (In fact, I have never raised sheep.) But, the Bible does have a lot to say about sheep. In Numbers chapter 27, God has led His people through the wilderness and they are closing in on the Promised Land. God informed Moses that Moses himself will not be entering the Promised Land, but he will get to see it. "Moses spoke to the Lord, saying, 'Let the Lord, the God of the spirits of all flesh, appoint a man over the congregation who shall go out before them and come in before them, who shall lead them out and bring them in, that the congregation of the Lord may not be as sheep that have no shepherd'" (Numbers 27:15-17). Moses just called God's people sheep that need a shepherd to lead them. In 1 Kings chapter 22, Micaiah says, "I saw all Israel scattered on the mountains, as sheep that have no shepherd" (1 Kings 22:17a). Psalm 100 says, "Know that the Lord, he is God! It is He who made us, and we are His; we are His people, and the sheep of His pasture" (Psalm 100:3). God so often refers to His people as sheep. You see this same idea echoed in the New Testament as well. God's people (you and I) are like sheep.

You have a basic flocking instinct—all people do.

What happens when a child gets hurt or scared? Most often they begin to cry and look for mom or dad. Why? They are looking for the place they know is safe. Has that changed in your life? I'm guessing it hasn't changed too much. When things are tough in your life, do you continue to open up and let people in or do you have to fight the urge to shut people out? Don't get angry at the question. Answer it honestly. (I'll be honest. I have a tendency, in hard times, to pull things in.) You bring in your inner circle—your trusted flock. You keep an eye on each other and keep outsiders out. This is called the flocking mentality. This mentality isn't necessarily wrong. The flocking mentality also makes you a natural born follower. You follow the older, wiser members of your flock. This means accepting their ideas, tendencies, behaviors, and beliefs. Again, this is not necessarily a bad thing. Everyone has to learn how to interact with people from somewhere. The expression "like father, like son" communicates this idea. Flocking is a basic instinct you were born with. You have to understand that the flocking instinct is a trait God gave you intentionally. The flocking instinct is what makes you dependent.

Beginning Dependent

Sheep need a protector. From the very beginning of

their lives, sheep need a leader. Sheep need a shepherd. Moses said he didn't want to see God's people "as sheep that have no shepherd" (Numbers 27:17b). Sheep that have no leader, or get separated from the flock, don't typically find their way home. Sheep don't act normal when separated from their flock. Sheep don't survive long when they are scattered. This is why a shepherd is so necessary for the good of the flock. If God's people are sheep, who is their shepherd? "For thus says the Lord God: Behold, I, I myself will search for my sheep and will seek them out" (Ezekiel 34:11). God goes on to say, "I myself will be the shepherd of my sheep" (Ezekiel 34:15a). God's desire for His people has always been to be their shepherd. God has always wanted to be their leader. From the very moment he called Abram from his father's house to "the land that I (God) will show you" (Genesis 12:1b, clarification mine). We see the image of God as the leader again when He delivered His people from Egypt. The people of Israel literally followed the pillar of cloud and pillar of fire that represented the presence of God. (Exodus 13:21-22.) When Abram set out from Haran he was depending on God to lead him. Abram wasn't sure where he was going or what to expect once he got there, but he went. When the people of Israel left Egypt, toward the wilderness, they didn't know exactly what was ahead, but they knew it was God who had delivered them from Pharaoh. Abram and the people of Israel were depending on God from the very beginning of their journeys. God had recognized them as His sheep. God had called His sheep, His people, by name and led His people from where He found them to where He wanted them to be. God was leading His people to a place that was best for them.

Following without knowing the exact destination is the sentiment of your life as you begin your walk following Christ. When you say "yes" to Jesus' call to follow after Him you have no idea where that path may lead, but you choose to trust and follow him. Just like the people of Israel did when God called them from where they were and led them to a new place, a good place that He had chosen for them. Just like sheep following a shepherd. Jesus uses the same description in John chapter 10. "He who enters by the door is the shepherd of the sheep. To him the gatekeeper opens. The sheep hear His voice, and He calls His own sheep by name and leads them out" (John 10:2-3). When you see it from this perspective, you can understand that Jesus wasn't talking about something new. Jesus didn't come into this world and suddenly make God's character change. God's character and love for His people had been established for thousands of years. God showed you physical examples of what His desire is for you. God's desire for you is to call you by name from where you are and to lead you out from there.

From the very beginning of your relationship with Jesus, you declare you're depending on him.

If separated from the flock, a sheep is lost. That sheep will continue to wander with no instinct to find its way back to the flock. As it wanders in the wild, separated from its flock, it has only one thing it can do—cry out for help. That cry from the sheep is a declaration that it needs help. That sheep needs to find the flock, or someone needs to come rescue it, before a predator finds the sheep. Your initial response in following Jesus is crying out to God, declaring yourself dependent with your words and sincerely meaning it in your heart. You cry out because you have been made aware that you are separated from Him. When you do this, you begin the process of following Jesus down the unfamiliar trail. You begin that journey of dependence. The beginning of following Christ is a declaration of dependence.

Greater Dependence

"When He saw the crowds, He had compassion for them, because they were harassed and helpless, like sheep without a shepherd" (Matthew 9:36). Jesus saw the people—He saw you—and was moved with compassion to bring them (you) close. Jesus, as the good shepherd, sees what God speaks of in Ezekiel chapter 34. "My sheep were scattered;

they wandered over all the mountains and on every high hill. My sheep were scattered over all the face of the earth, with none to search or seek for them" (Ezekiel 34:6). When you were scattered and lost, by leading yourself, Jesus saw you. Jesus saw how helpless and lost you were on your own and He was moved with compassion. Jesus knew the price He would have to pay for you and He willing chose to pay full price for your freedom. Jesus purchased you with His own life. And that same Jesus—that paid the highest price for your life—has called you by name. Jesus saved you. It is because of Him that you are made new. It wasn't the prayer you prayed; it wasn't the words of a sermon you heard. "For by grace you have been saved through faith. And this is not your own doing; it is the gift of God" (Ephesians 2:8). Paul's words to the Ephesians declare that salvation is a gift of grace from God. Not only that, but even the faith you had to believe in Jesus is a gift from God. Ephesians 2 goes on to say, "Not a result of works, so that no one may boast" (Ephesians 2:9). God did the work needed for your salvation as an act of grace and love. He gave you the gift of faith to believe in Him so that you would have nothing to celebrate except for Him. When you said "yes" to Jesus, it was through dependence on the leadership of God.

Since your relationship with Jesus began through dependence, it is no shock that the further you follow Jesus the more dependent on Him you become. The longer you follow Jesus, the less you should depend on your own reasoning. Proverbs tells us, "Trust in the Lord with all your heart, and do not lean on your own understanding" (Proverbs 3:5). Faith is trusting in God, whom you cannot see. Living your life of faith is a daily act of dependence on Jesus Christ. "For we walk by faith, not by sight" (2 Corinthians 5:7). Your walk down the unfamiliar trail is one of trusting in the God of Abraham and Moses as He leads you into places you would never have imagined to go. As God leads you in ways that are contrary to human reason, you must be completely convinced and trust in God's voice and His leadership. You must be assured in your heart that the direction you are going is God's direction. This assurance and trust is necessary because you can be certain that following that path is not easy.

The path you are following Jesus down is the unfamiliar path for a reason. It's not common. It is not easy or comfortable. Just take a look at Jesus' wilderness experience in Luke chapter 4. "And Jesus, full of the Holy Spirit, returned from the Jordan and was *led by the Spirit in the wilderness* for forty days, being tempted by the devil. And He ate nothing during those days. And when they were ended, He was hungry" (Luke 4:1-2, emphasis mine). Matthew chapter 4 also makes the statement, "Jesus was *led up by the*

Spirit into the wilderness to be tempted by the devil" (Matthew 4:1, emphasis mine). Jesus, the son of God Himself, was led by the Holy Spirit—who is God—INTO the wilderness. Jesus didn't just decide to go into the wilderness and not eat for 40 days to show His devotion to God. Jesus was led by the Spirit into the wilderness. Jesus Himself walked down the unfamiliar path. Jesus' experience in the wilderness was just as hard as your experience is, or will be. Jesus' wilderness was filled with temptations from the devil, and yours will be too. His wilderness experience was a result of following the lead of the Holy Spirit, following the leadership of God (His shepherd), and yours should be too. Jesus' wilderness experience did not make Him more physically strong. I don't know if you have ever spent forty days not eating, but I can assure you that Jesus was tired and hungry. When you are tired and hungry, would you consider yourself stronger or weaker physically? Weaker, right? Jesus was physically weaker after forty days of not eating AND He was being tempted by the devil. The temptations and attacks from the devil weren't done. The Bible tells us that Jesus was tempted directly three more times. In response to these temptations, Jesus does NOT lean on His own understanding and try to reason with the devil. He does not stand up and wrestle with the devil to prove His abundant strength. Jesus doesn't barter with the devil or begin praying and trying to make a deal with

God to deliver Him out of temptation. He responds to the temptations of the devil by quoting the book of Deuteronomy. Jesus depends on the Word of God to deliver Him from these temptations. He had complete faith in the Word of God to deliver Him and not to leave Him helpless. Jesus, in His physical weakness, showed you the importance of depending on God and trusting in the Word of the Lord.

Your time in the wilderness will lead you into situations that are hard. Your walk down the unfamiliar trail will lead you into places where you are physically weak in order for you to see the strength of God's Word. God is leading you further through the wilderness, and into a relationship with Him, for you to exercise your faith. Your faith will grow and you will see your life reflect greater dependence on Jesus every day. God is not leading you into the wilderness for you to trust your wealth. He is not leading you down the unfamiliar trail for you to trust in your own understanding. God is calling you to trust Him. Jesus has called you to follow Him. Jesus is leading you in a way that will require greater trust—greater faith—greater dependence.

Interdependence

As you follow Jesus down the unfamiliar trail, you don't walk alone. You are following Jesus, you have been given the

Holy Spirit, and you have other followers of Christ walking the trail with you. Jesus says narrow is the way and there are *few* people who find it. Few, meaning more than one, but not everyone. There will be others on the unfamiliar trail with you; they are followers of God and part of the body of Christ, the church. "For as in one body we have many members, and the members do not all have the same function, so we, though many, are one body in Christ, and individually members one of another" (Romans 12:4-5). We are one body! You are inter-connected in Christ with other followers of Christ. There are several commands in scripture that involve "one another." The Bible says to love one another (Romans 12:10), encourage one another (1 Thessalonians 4:18), forgive one another (Ephesians 4:32), live in harmony with one another (Romans 12:16), instruct one another (Romans 15:14), and there are many more examples. The key to one another is that there is at least one and another. Jesus Himself even said, "By this all people will know that you are my disciples, if you have love for one another" (John 13:35). As you follow God into greater levels of dependence, you should find yourself more connected to the body of Christ. You cannot remove yourself from a community of believers and still consider yourself a follower of Christ, while not following the commands of scripture concerning one another. The Bible is very clear concerning connection with other believers. It does not give you an out. The desire to separate is from your nature of sin and not from the nature of the new man, or woman, God has made you to be.

If Jesus has called you by name, you have been made new. Your strength is in numbers, just like the strength of the sheep is in the flock. The Bible says, "And let us consider how to stir up one another to love and good works, not neglecting to meet together, as is the habit of some, but encouraging one another, and all the more as you see the Day drawing near" (Hebrews□ □10:24-25). The flock encourages one another toward the things of God. The flock (the body of Christ) gives strength to you and helps you to continue following Jesus until the day He comes again for His own people. Until you are delivered from this life, through physical death, it is a command of scripture to be interdependent on other believers in your journey down the unfamiliar trail.

If you are a follower of Christ and are attempting to live out your faith disconnected from a community of believers, repent. Ask God to forgive you and trust Him to lead you into a community of believers that are walking the unfamiliar trail as well. Get connected to a Bible-believing, Jesus-following church that is preaching the truth of God's word and encouraging you, teaching you, challenging you, and pointing you toward Jesus Christ.

CHAPTER 7
WORSHIP

Greater dependence is characterized by sacrifice. According to the New Oxford American Dictionary, sacrifice is "an act of surrendering a possession as an offering to God. An act of giving up something valued for the sake of something else regarded as more important or worthy."[11] Sacrifice is worship. Sacrifice can seem intimidating, because it communicates an idea of being costly. There are costs involved in both sacrifice and worship. The reality of sacrifice (and worship) is, if it doesn't cost you anything, it probably doesn't qualify as a sacrifice (or worship.) Sacrifice is an act of giving up something valued just as an offering must be something of value. David communicated this in 2

Samuel chapter 24 when he said, "I will not offer burnt offering to the Lord my God that cost me nothing" (2 Samuel 24:24b). Sacrifice and worship involve giving up something of value.

Something of Value

What makes things valuable? Is it just the monetary price or is there more to it than that? It doesn't take long in life to understand that value is not just determined by monetary cost, although that is one way value is recognized. There is so much more to value than just money. Let's look at a few ways value is recognized.

Power & Authority

The power or authority trusted to someone or something makes it valuable. For example, the CEO of a fortune 500 company will undoubtedly have a higher salary than an entry-level employee. This makes sense because the responsibility and expectation of the two are vastly different. The CEO is responsible for the entire company. The CEO is held accountable for the production, profitability, morale, and functionality of the company. An entry-level employee is only responsible for fulfilling their duties. The CEO has meetings, initiatives, and communications with employees, supervisors, managers, partners, executives, and investors. The entry-level employee comes to work, performs their duties, and keeps the boss happy. The CEO has the authority to hire and fire anyone he chooses or deems necessary. The entry-level employee doesn't hire or fire anyone. It is abundantly clear that, to the company, the CEO is of more value than the entry-level employee and it is confirmed not just through money but in power and authority that was trusted to him or her.

This is not a new principle that we, in our finite wisdom, came up with. This principle of value, being recognized through power and authority, actually comes from God. Genesis tells the story of creation. In Genesis chapter 1, God creates everything in single days. And at the end of every day God said it was good. "And God saw that it was good. And there was evening and there was morning, the fourth day" (Genesis 1:18b-19). On days five and six, God creates things on the earth and He blessed them to, "Be fruitful and multiply" (Genesis 1:22, 28). But on day six there is one thing that is peculiar that God says and does. "Then God said, 'Let us make man in our image, after our likeness. And let them have dominion" (Genesis 1:26a). Then God said to man, "Be fruitful and multiply and fill all the earth and *subdue it, and have dominion* over the fish of the sea and over the birds of the heavens and over every living thing that moves on the earth" (Genesis 1:28, emphasis mine). This is unusual because the creator of the universe, on day six of creation, gives authority over the entire earth to man. God recognized the value of man not only in making him different from all the rest of creation, "in our image, after our likeness" (Genesis 1:26), but God showed the value of man above all other creations by trusting man with the authority over all the earth and everything on the earth that moves. Man and woman alike were trusted with this authority. You were trusted with this authority. You were recognized as more valuable than any of God's other creations through the authority and power that God trusted to man from the beginning of time.

Time & Effort

Power and authority are not the only way things are recognized as valuable. The time and effort something requires recognizes it as valuable as well. There are two examples that come to mind for me. The first example is the restoration of a classic car. You go to the junkyard and find the shell of 1950's model pickup. It has an engine in it, but it doesn't run. It has some rusted parts, flat tires, and it is even missing the seat. You don't see a piece of junk; you see an opportunity. After all, one man's trash is another man's treasure. You buy it, take it home, and put it in the garage. Every weekend you work on one specific part of this overwhelming project. Your first weekend is focused on organizing everything and knowing exactly what you have. The next weekend you work on collecting the parts that you need. Then you spend time repairing the body. Next, the engine and transmission. After that, the bed and the interior design. Finally, you get to the point that you can begin polishing all of the finish work while you send the truck off to get the right paint job. When you get it all put together, after two and a half years' worth of weekends, you have the reality of the dream you saw in the junk yard. Your wife tells you it's time to move it out of the garage so she can have her parking spot back and you decide it's a necessary point of discussion. Why the resistance? Because your time and effort invested in the fully refurbished 1950's pickup recognizes it as very valuable. To you, that pickup now has greater value than the $20,000 SUV your wife drives.

Raising kids is another clear example of time and effort recognizing value. You spend at least 18 years of their lives caring for them. You make sure they have food, clothing, and shelter. You spend nights holding them as they cry themselves to sleep. You get up in the middle of the night to feed them when they are babies. You get up in the middle of the night to calm them down when they have a bad dream. You coach their little league team. You learn all their cheers for cheerleading, whether you want to or not. You celebrate their accomplishments. You correct them when it is necessary. You give them time to talk through problems and help them understand the right responses. Even after they are gone from your home, you make time for them. You make sure they have food and clothing and even money. After all, they are your children. They are valuable to you. You have recognized and shown them they are valuable through your time and effort.

God did this with His own children. "Thus says the Lord, Israel is my firstborn son" (Exodus 4:22b). God has invested in and provided for His people for more than 4,000 years. God leads His children out the slavery of Egypt. God establishes a relationship with His children in the wilderness. God sets His children apart from all other people of the world. God gives His people the land of Canaan that was actually occupied by several people groups already. God spent nearly 2,000 years speaking to them through prophets before He sends Jesus to be with His people. Then Jesus changed everything—He gave all people access to God. God is known as the Father. In 1 John, God's Word says, "See what kind of love the Father has given to us, that we should be called *children of God*" (1 John 3:1a, emphasis mine). God called you His child and He invests His time and effort into you to recognize your value. God doesn't just invest a year or two into you; God invests your lifetime worth of time and effort to restore you and maintain you in relationship with Jesus. God's effort and time invested in you recognizes your value, not just today, but for all eternity. God's desire is that you have life—eternal life—and there is no amount of time or effort that He has not exhausted to recognize your value.

Price Paid

The term "you get what you pay for" definitely applies to value. My first car was a four door Geo Metro that I shared with my twin brother, Kyle. My parents bought it from an auto auction through a friend of our family. The car wasn't new. It wasn't very expensive, but we were in high school and it got us from home to school and pretty much everywhere else we needed to go. The Geo was awesome on gas, not so great on power. Kyle and I wouldn't take it out on the interstate because it didn't have enough power to maintain speed going uphill. For what we needed it to do, it was a decent car. I wouldn't necessarily buy it again, but it was my first car. I wasn't exactly sure how much my parents paid for it but I knew it wasn't much.

When Kyle and I had graduated high school and were going to college, it wasn't manageable to share a car anymore. Kyle got mom's old car, mom took our old car, and I (with the help of my parents) bought a Chevy S-10 pickup. It wasn't the fanciest and nicest truck I could buy, but it was much nicer than the car I had driven in high school. This time I knew exactly how much it cost because I was making the payment. I wouldn't say I neglected the Geo Metro, but I valued the truck a lot more. I kept the truck cleaner. I made sure the oil was changed on time. I was more careful about where I parked and how I drove. Why? Because I knew how much the truck cost. I recognized the truck to be more valuable than the car by the price I paid for the truck.

God declared value to you much like Hosea did for Gomer. "And the Lord said to me, 'Go again, love a woman who is loved by another man and is an adulteress, even as the Lord loves the children of Israel, though they turn to other gods and love cakes of raisins.' So I bought her for fifteen shekels of silver and a homer and a lethech of barley" (Hosea 3:1-2). Hosea just paid full price for Gomer. Hosea recognized Gomer's value as a complete and whole wife. Hosea didn't negotiate to pay a discounted price for her. Hosea wasn't recognizing the value of Gomer as she was, but he paid the price for Gomer that recognized her as the most valuable of all. God directed Hosea in this. God used Hosea to communicate, in part, what Jesus would do completely.

God sent His son, Jesus, who lived the same life we live and did not sin. "One who in every respect has been tempted as we are, yet without sin" (Hebrews 4:15b). Jesus knows your weaknesses; He understands your failures. Jesus knows that you have rejected Him from birth, but He didn't use that as an excuse to negotiate the value of your life. Jesus didn't barter with God over the price to recognize your value. Instead, Jesus willingly gave up His life, through death on a cross, so that through His blood you would be able to recognize just how valuable you are. Jesus, the son of God, who gave all the power and authority to man, paid the price of His life to show the value of your life. God paid the price that recognized you as the most valuable of all creation. Through God's great gift of mercy and grace, He is getting, and will get, what He paid for.

The Act of Giving Up

God has shown through the entire Bible that you are valuable; more valuable than any other creation. Your life has unimaginable value to God. Every part of your life has that type of value to God. Your thoughts, your actions, your finances, your house, your cars, your family, your heart, everything about you. Everything associated with you is valuable to God. God paid full price for you. God has invested incredible time and effort to make Himself known to you. God has trusted you with incredible power and authority. Jesus calls you to deny yourself and follow Him. (Luke 9:23.) God did this to show you how valuable you are, so that you would have something of value to willingly give up. In order to truly sacrifice—in order to truly worship God—you have to give up something valuable. You do not have anything of value to God except your life. Romans chapter 12 says, "I appeal to you therefore, brothers, by the mercies of God, to present *your bodies* as a *living sacrifice*, holy and acceptable to God, which is your *spiritual worship*" (Romans 12:1, emphasis mine). Present YOUR BODIES as a LIVING SACRIFICE! When you choose to live this life, surrendered to God and walking with Him down the unfamiliar trail, you will have to fight the desire to be in control. As you follow Jesus, willingly giving up your only thing of value, you declare Jesus as more important. Your life surrendered to God, as a living sacrifice, shows God that you value Him more than anything you have.

Worship is not just singing songs. Worship is not just giving in an offering. Worship is a life completely surrendered to God. Worship is giving up everything of value in your life for the sake of following Jesus. When you give up everything of value in your life, songs of joy over flow from you. When you trust God completely, giving God your money isn't a question. When you are committed to worshipping God through giving up your life, God will take care of the rest. "Seek first the kingdom of God and His righteousness, and all these things will be added to you" (Matthew 6:33).

CHAPTER 8
THE LAND OF PROMISE

The people of Israel had followed God throughout the wilderness for forty years. God had appointed Joshua to lead the people in Moses' place. They were positioned on the edge of the wilderness and only the Jordan River was between Israel and the Promised Land. "Then Joshua rose early in the morning and they set out from Shittim. And they came to the Jordan, he and all the people of Israel, and lodged there before they passed over" (Joshua 3:1). It was finally time to follow God into the Promised Land. "Now the priests bearing the ark of the covenant of the Lord stood firmly on dry ground in the midst of the Jordan, and all Israel was passing over on dry ground until all the nation finished passing over the Jordan" (Joshua 3:17). God had led His people to the Promised Land just as He said e would. God never left the people of Israel in the wilderness. God never abandoned them on the unfamiliar trail. God has made the same promise to you as well. God told Joshua directly, "Just as I was with Moses, so I will be with you. I will not leave you or forsake you" (Joshua 1:5b). God communicates the same thing repeatedly to Joshua and the people of Israel about entering the Promised Land. Along with the words, "Be strong and courageous" (Deuteronomy 31:6a).

There are some things that you have to know about entering the Promised Land. This Promised Land is not empty. The Promised Land that God is leading you toward will require you to be courageous in following God's commands. You will need to have a strong and steadfast faith in Jesus. You are going to need to remember what God has done to get you to the Promised Land.

Remembering

"When all the nation had finished passing over the Jordan, the Lord said to Joshua, 'Take twelve men from the people, from each tribe a man, and command them saying, "Take twelve stones from here out of the midst of the Jordan"'" (Joshua 4:1-3a). God had pushed back the waters of the Jordan River so that His people could walk from the wilderness into the Promised Land. On their way across the dry ground, God told Joshua to have twelve large stones collected from the river. Why do God's people need these big rocks? "When your children ask in time to come, 'What do those stones mean to you?' then you shall tell them" (Joshua 4:6b-7a). "These stones shall be to the people of Israel a memorial forever" (Joshua 4:7b). God was giving His people something to remember this event by. God just gave His people a grandparent story-telling opportunity. These twelve large stones were stacked together, so kids would ask, "Hey grandpa! What's that?" And then grandpa, remembering having walked across that dry ground, would tell of the power of God that brought His people to this place they now call home. It would be an opportunity to share the testimony of what God had done. As you follow Jesus, and He leads you into your Promised Land, there are some things you will need to remember. There are some stones of memorial you need to carry with you forever.

In our home, we have literal rocks. These small river rocks have been written on with a marker. They represent things we, as a family, have believed God for and prayed for. When God answers, we write a date on that rock so that we can talk about the things God has done in our lives. We also have trinkets, keepsakes and collectibles from different adventures and times in our lives. We have keepsakes from my trip to Ukraine. We each have something from Kenya that was brought to us from a friend, named Lauren, who followed Jesus and spent a month there. We have pine cones from Colorado Springs to remember our time there and the many things God did in and through us. All these things are a reminder to us of who God is and where He has led us. We remember God and have them out in our home so that when people see them and ask "What's that?" we can answer with the stories of what God did.

You should have these things as well. I encourage you, as you follow Jesus down the unfamiliar trail, to write your journey down in a journal. Take rocks you've written on and pray over them. When God does something significant in your life, pick up something as a reminder of what God has done. Give yourself a reason to talk about who God is and to remember the work God has done to bring you to where you are today. Remember that Revelation chapter 12 tells you that you overcome the devil by the blood of Jesus and the word of our testimony. (Revelation 12:11.) You overcome the enemy when you remember and talk about: what God has done in your life, how the Holy Spirit has given you wisdom when you needed it, when Jesus helped you overcome addiction, God healing you from sickness. When you talk about how God used you to communicate His love for others and they said "yes" to following Jesus—you are sharing your testimony! You are conquering the devil and declaring Jesus as Lord! You are living in the freedom of Jesus by continuing to remember Him.

This is the heart of God for the Promised Land—living in freedom! When you remember Jesus, and share your testimony, you are choosing the freedom of Jesus. "So if the Son sets you free, you will be free indeed" (John 8:36). When you live this way continually, no matter where you are, you are free in Christ. You are free from the slavery of sin, free to live in relationship with God, and no longer influenced by your surroundings. You truly can live life the way Jesus intended when He said, "They are not of this world, just as I am not of the world. Sanctify them in the truth; your word is truth. As you have sent me into the world, so I have sent them into the world" (John 17:16-18). You, not being of this world, are led by the truth—which is Jesus Christ—to tell the world about God's work in your life. You can't tell people about what God has done if you don't remember it yourself.

Take Possession

"Joshua commanded the officers of the people, 'Pass through the midst of the camp and command the people, 'Prepare your provisions, for within three days you are to pass over this Jordan to go in to take possession of the land that the Lord your God is giving you to possess'" (Joshua 1:10-11). God was sending the people of Israel into their Promised Land to take possession of it. They had to take possession of it because there were already people settled there. I find it very interesting that God sent His people to a land that was already occupied. God could have chosen any place to send Israel, but He chose this land because He promised it to Abraham (Abram), the father of Israel. Why is the best land always taken?—because it's the best. God doesn't want His people to settle for second rate. God paid the highest price for you and He wants you to have His promise, not some version of it. God wants you to enter His Promised Land, not settle for land in the wilderness. (See chapter 5.) In order to take possession of the Promised Land of God, there will be a fight or two (or several). But these fights are different than the ones you fought in the wilderness.

In the wilderness, Israel had no fortified cities and the people who opposed this group of wanderers came out against them. Your enemy doesn't want to see you reach your Promised Land. Your enemy wants to strike fear into you. Your enemy wants to steal your promise from God and scare you into giving up on following God completely. That's the fight in the wilderness, but in the Promised Land the fight is against fortified cities. Just look at Jericho.

Archaeologists tell us that the ancient city was surrounded by two walls; the inner wall being some four meters (13 feet) wide and the outer wall being two meters (6.5 feet) wide, estimated to have been about nine meters (29.5 feet) high.[12] That is a massive protective wall between the people of Jericho and anyone who might attack them. Joshua had led the people of Israel into battles in the wilderness, but he had to recognize this fight was different than the ones before. My honest opinion is that there was no physical way the people of Israel were able to win this fight. I believe that Jericho would have outlasted any and all the strength the people of Israel had to offer.

That's a key difference in the wilderness and the Promised Land: in the wilderness, YOU have to fight to survive, but in the Promised Land, GOD is the one doing the fighting. "When Joshua was by Jericho, he lifted up his eyes and looked, and behold, a man was standing before him with his sword in his hand. And Joshua went to him and said to him, 'Are you for us, or for our adversaries?' And he said, 'No; but I am the commander of the army of the Lord. Now I have come'" (Joshua 5:13-14a). First, I have to point out how brave Joshua was to walk up to a man he didn't know who had a sword in his hand. Next, you have to understand that God sent the commander of His army to fight. We aren't told of any commander of the army of the Lord showing up in the wilderness, but this is the Promised Land. God always makes good on His promises. God is truth; He cannot lie. When God speaks it, it exists. (See Genesis chapters 1-3.) The battle has changed now. The Promised Land's first battle plan was not one taught at any military academy. (Joshua 6.) Here's the plan! You seven priests take these horns and stand right here—you guys are going to be in front. Next, the Ark of the Covenant, which represents the presence of God, will be carried. Behind the Ark of the Covenant is where everyone else will be. Now that we have our positions, we are going to walk around the city one time every day for six days. No one is going to make a noise during these trips around the city. The priests will blow the trumpets and the rest of us are going to be completely quiet on the entire march. The only sound they will hear is our footsteps. We are going to do that for six days.

On the seventh day, we will walk around the city seven times, and after we have finished the seventh lap, the priests will blow the trumpets with a loud, long sound. When you hear that long, loud blast, you are going to shout with everything you've got. When everyone shouts together on the seventh day, the wall of the city is going to fall down flat. Once it does, you go up and destroy everything in the city, "But all silver and gold, and every vessel of bronze and iron, are holy to the Lord; they shall go into the treasury of the Lord" (Joshua 6:19).

A 20 foot thick, double wall of stone doesn't just fall down by chance at the same time the people of God are standing outside the city, shouting as loud as they can. This was a battle completely won by the hand of God. And to the victor go the spoils. God told the people of Israel not to take the precious things of Jericho, but to surrender them to the treasury of the Lord. These precious and valuable things would represent the spoils of victory. These spoils, or keepsakes, would have been things the warriors who fought in the battle were normally entitled to keep for themselves. Traditionally, this was part of the compensation a soldier would receive for their service in the battle. Much of these spoils would have been used to pay for everyday expenses once they got home or maybe even on the trip home. Some of these things would be collected and displayed, much like the memorial stones we talked about previously. They would have been reminders and conversational pieces, trophies of sorts. The warriors who fought would have surely had them to tell the stories of their accomplishments. But in this particular battle, God said to give all the spoils to His treasury. I believe this is to represent that God did all the work in this battle. At Jericho, God had won the fight all on His own and the people of Israel were going to willingly surrender the spoils of war to the only warrior who did any fighting.

God fought the battle of Jericho for his people, just like God will fight your battles in your Promised Land. Your battles aren't the same any more. They aren't won by strength, but by God himself. In this land you are given the promise, "Every place that the sole of your foot will tread upon I have given to you, just as I promised Moses" (Joshua 1:3). In the land that God has promised you, you will walk in victory. You are led by the truth, declaring the goodness of Jesus in your life, allowing God to fight your battles for you. When God goes before you and fights your battles, there is no doubt you will take possession of your Land of Promise.

Your Eternal Promised Land

"When the Son of Man comes in His glory, and all the angels with Him, then He will sit on His glorious throne. Before Him will be gathered all the nations, and He will separate people one from another as a shepherd separates sheep from the goats. And He will place the sheep on His right, but the goats on the left. Then the King will say to those on His right, 'Come, you who are blessed by my Father, inherit the kingdom prepared for you from the foundation of the world'" (Matthew 25:31-34). These are the words of Jesus in Matthew chapter 25. Jesus is coming back to get His people one day. Jesus is coming back to get His faithful followers: not passive followers who said a prayer one time and then lived life their own way. Jesus is coming back for His people who know Him and He knows them. One day Jesus is returning and you will stand before Him and He will either count you as a sheep who followed Him or a goat who rejected Him. There are no other options. If you are a sheep, a true follower of Jesus, then Jesus says the kingdom of inheritance—that He has prepared from the beginning of time—is yours. If you follow God faithfully (completely) down the unfamiliar trail, you will find eternal life in the presence of God. "And I saw the holy city, New Jerusalem, coming down out of heaven from God, prepared as a bride adorned for her husband. And I heard a loud voice from the throne saying, 'Behold, the dwelling place of God is with man. He will dwell with them, and they will be his people, and God himself will be with them as their God. He will wipe away every tear from their eyes, and death shall be no more, neither shall there be mourning, nor crying, nor pain anymore, for the former things have passed away'" (Revelation 21:2-4).

God's eternal promises will be fulfilled at the end of time. The shadow and symbol of your earthly Promised Land will be fully complete. With no more fear of death, no more pain, no more invisible God. You will live in the physical, eternal presence of God in the New Jerusalem. This is your eternal Promised Land, what is called our Blessed Hope, the returning of Jesus Christ to take his people into the physical presence of God. This is where the story ends and eternity begins for followers of Jesus.

Have you chosen to follow God completely, all the days of your life? If not, will you? If you have, be bold and take that first step onto the unfamiliar trail. Truly be a fully-devoted follower of Jesus! What are you waiting for? Let's go!

Sources

1. Unless otherwise noted, all scripture quotations are from The ESV Bible (The Holy Bible, English Standard Version), copyright 2001 by crossway, a publishing ministry of Good News Publishers. Used by permission. All rights reserved.
2. Scripture quotations marked (NKJV) are from the New King James Version.
   Copyright 1982 by Thomas Nelson, Inc. Used by permission. All rights reserved.
3. Scripture quotations marked (NIV) are from the HOLY BIBLE, NEW INTERNATIONAL VERSION Copyright 1973, 1978, 1984 International Bible Society. Used by permission of Zondervan Bible Publishers.
4. Dr. Todd Hudnall, "The Brazen Laver," Part 3 of the God's Mobile Home Series, Colorado Springs, CO. July 13th, 2014
5. Peter F. Dorman, "Egyptian religion". *Encyclopædia Britannica. Encyclopædia Britannica Online.* Encyclopædia Britannica Inc., 2016. Web. 12 Feb. 2016 <http://www.britannica.com/topic/Egyptian-religion>.
6. Scripture quotations marked (KJV) are from *The Holy Bible*, King James Version. Public Domain.
7. Rise of the Guardians. Dir. Peter Ramsey Perf. Chris Pine, Hugh Jackman, Jude Law, and Alec Baldwin. DreamWorks, 2012. DVD.
8. Scripture quotations marked (AMP) are from The Amplified Bible. Copyright 2015 by The Lockman Foundation. Used by permission. (www.Lockman.org)
9. Biography.com Editors, "Martin Luther Biography". *A&E Television Networks. The Biography.com website.* Web. 12 Feb. 2016
<*http://www.biography.com/people/martin-luther-9389283*>

10. Susan Schoenian, "Sheep 201: A Beginners Guide to Raising Sheep, Sheep Behavior" *Susan Schoenian.* Copyright 2014. Web. 12 Feb. 2016
<*http://www.sheep101.info/201/behavior.html*>

11. New Oxford American Dictionary. Eds. Stevenson, Angus, and Christine A. Lindberg. : Oxford University Press, 2010. Oxford Reference. 2011. Date Accessed 12 Feb. 2016
<http://www.oxfordreference.com/view/10.1093/acref/9780195392883.001.0001/acref-9780195392883>.

12. Unknown Author "Jericho". N.P. Web. 12 Feb. 2016
<http://www.biblebasics.co.uk/natcit/jericho.htm>

13. Schaefer, Glenn. E. "Repent." *Baker's Evangelical Dictionary of Biblical Theology*. Ed.
Walter A. Elwell. Grand Rapids: Baker Books, 1996. *Bible Study Tools Online.* Web. 11 Feb. 2016
<http://www.biblestudytools.com/lexicons/greek/nas/metanoeo.html>

ABOUT THE AUTHOR

Kirk Jackson is the husband to Chelsie and together they have three wonderful kids: Nicolas, Lauryn, and Sawyer Grace. Kirk leans on his experience in vocational ministry and organizational leadership to communicate the realities of the planned and unplanned transitions in life. The Jacksons have experienced life in Oklahoma, Texas, and Colorado. They currently live in Oklahoma.

www.ingramcontent.com/pod-product-compliance
Lightning Source LLC
LaVergne TN
LVHW010621100826
845148LV00014B/3064
* 9 7 8 0 6 9 2 6 8 2 6 0 9 *